SOUTH WEST HARBOURS
Ships & Trades

Michael Langley

MP Middleton Press

Front cover pictures:
 top left - see caption 203
 top right - see caption 180
 middle left - see caption 10
 bottom - see caption 105

Back cover pictures:
 top - see caption 111
 bottom - see caption 120

Notes about the Author-

Born in West Sussex, the interest in coastal shipping began from around the age of twelve when, armed with a simple camera, visits to the local harbours began. Cross Solent journeys to the Family's other stronghold, the Isle of Wight, were further enticement to embark upon a career at sea. A year was spent at Navigation School before joining the P & O Group Company, Trident Tankers Ltd., as a navigating cadet. Some twenty six years later whilst serving as a Marine Superintendent in Ship Management at Head Office, redundancy materialised. A move to the Isle of Wight rekindled the interest in coastal shipping history and research, and this book follows on from - 'SUSSEX SHIPPING - Sail, Steam and Motor', 'SOLENT- Creeks, Craft & Cargoes', and 'KENT SEAWAYS - Hoys to Hovercraft'.

Published February 2008

ISBN 978 1 906008 22 2

© *Middleton Press, 2008*

Design Deborah Esher

Published by
 Middleton Press
 Easebourne Lane
 Midhurst
 West Sussex
 GU29 9AZ
Tel: 01730 813169
Fax: 01730 812601
Email: info@middletonpress.co.uk
www.middletonpress.co.uk

Printed & bound by Biddles Ltd, Kings Lynn

CONTENTS

PREFACE

The carriage of goods by sea today is, for an island nation, as important as ever. Sailing ships, steam ships and the now ubiquitous motor ships have all played their vital role, together with harbour development to facilitate expanding trades. This book examines the many ship types seen in and around the West Country ports over the last century or so. Some historical background notes are included to highlight continuing harbour improvements and certain specific trades. Some recent photographs endeavour to afford the reader modern comparison views of once busy industrial locations.

GLOSSARY & ABBREVIATIONS

....	Sailing Ships / un-powered craft	MV	Motor Vessel	ST	Steam Tug
MB	Motor barge	PS	Paddle Steamer	TSS	Twin Screw Steam Ship
MFV	Motor Fishing Vessel	SS	Steam Ship	TSMV	Twin Screw Motor Vessel
MT	Motor Tanker / Motor Tug				

Tonnages:

Gross Registered Tonnage, abbr. grt;-g- volumetric measure of all enclosed space applied to all ships. 100cu. ft. = 1 gross ton. This is the true indicator of the ship's overall physical size.

Net Registered Tonnage, abbr. nrt;-n- sometimes shown as reg. tons, -r- probable derivation from sailing ship days in the wine trade when 'tun' implied barrel capacity of 252 gallons. The number of barrels carried thus giving earning capacity volume.

Deadweight Tonnage, abbr. dwt;-d- the actual weight carrying capacity of the ship in tons, including fuel, water, stores etc., plus cargo.

Tons 'burthen' or 'burden'- an early statement of 'deadweight' used for cargo vessels in the 17th and 18th centuries.

Forms used in this book-eg., 199g / 1960..... a ship of 199 tons gross built in 1960.

Length overall:	loa	Measurement to the fore and aft extremities.
Beam or breadth:	br.	Measurement to the maximum width
Draught:	dr.	Depth of water required for flotation
L.A.D:		Low air draught- (ship type)

Horse Power, engines:-
np Nominal Horse Power
ihp Indicated Horse Power
shp Shaft Horse Power - usually given for steam ships.
bhp Brake Horse Power - usually given for motor ships.
psi Boiler pressure in lbs. per square inch.

Knots/kts: Speed in nautical miles (6080ft) per hour.

Spring Tides: Fortnightly periods of greater tidal range- 'higher' high water and 'lower' low water.

Neap Tides: Intervening periods of lesser tidal range- 'lower' high water and 'higher' low water.

INTRODUCTION

A thousand years ago sailing vessels were tiny and most 'ports' consisted simply of landing places, often little better than open beaches or at best, within the more sheltered estuaries. Yet traffic in people and goods had already existed for millennia. As rudimentary ship construction techniques improved, open craft became 'decked over', thereby affording some weather protection. The seamanship and navigational skills of the old time seafarer cannot be overestimated, for they sailed 'point by point' close to the land whenever possible. Their hard earned knowledge of tides, currents, weather patterns and the capabilities of their own vessels, enabled running ashore at the right time to load or unload on a shelving beach, commonplace. Of course there were enormous risks and inevitable mishaps, yet this kind of operation was accomplished as a matter of routine, and trade flourished.

The West Country and Cornwall in particular was blessed with an abundance of various mineral deposits, extracted to some extent for centuries before the industrial revolution. However, it would be that accelerating process and the need for coal to power steam machinery that would witness sea trade's rapid expansion. Ores could now be readily shipped away to growing industrial areas such as South Wales for refining and processing. Roads were mainly of little use, often little better than tracks, unsafe to use and incapable of shifting any weight or volume of goods by horse drawn cart. The burgeoning railway network of the mid 1800s made an impact on inland goods movement but on balance probably encouraged more sea trade as sidings were quickly built to connect wharves, quays and docks to the rail system. Coastal shipping would continue to prosper until road haulage and 'through' containerised traffic siphoned away most freight by the 1980s, excepting bulk commodities.

The arrival of the steamships in the early 1800s and motorships just a century later after WWI, would put reliability into sailing schedules, yet reliance on the old 'wind power' would die out only very slowly. The new motorships took several decades to completely replace the steamers - they had an extended stay of execution by virtue of fuel oil replacing coal for bunkers. Ship owners had always rather begrudged the degree of space required for coal bunkers since it reduced cargo capacity. By the 1960s the remaining steam powered coastal vessels could no longer compete against the motor vessels. Ironically, the installation of oil engines as auxiliary motors for sailing vessels after WWI enabled many an old wooden hull to compete with more modern tonnage, in some cases right up to the 1960s.

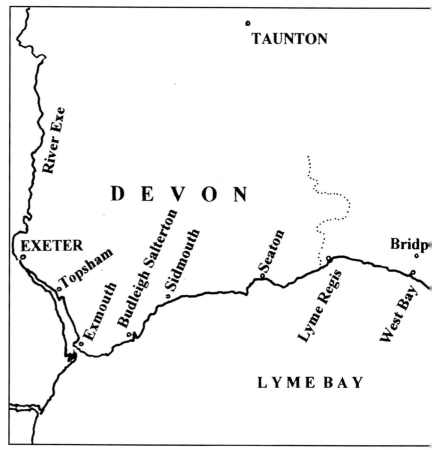

4

With relentless growth of industry, ship sizes individually increased in carrying capacity, and deep water harbours became essential to service them. The search for 'economy of scale in operation' has been ever present in seaborne trade. A century ago, small ships required large crews to operate them, yet carried relatively little cargo. Today, enormous vessels manned by small crews carry unimaginably large volumes of cargo, worldwide. Such ships can, of course only operate to the larger deepwater harbours with infrastructure suitable to handle them. Sadly this has seen the demise of commercial shipping to all but a handful of small ports.

The development of 'modern ports' as we know them today around England appears to have taken a major leap forward about 1600, when a new degree of commercialisation and improved building techniques allowed stone pier construction in earnest. Every small harbour thus improved could then offer shelter and the services required by shipping. A number also developed local ship building facilities. Breakwaters, piers, jetties, locks, docks and even drydocks would for evermore have to keep pace with larger and larger ships. The notion 'afloat at all times' came into common parlance from the marine insurance industry - this pre-requisite would ensure avoidance of grounding stresses when loading or unloading. The true coastal ships of today still have to sit aground whilst handling cargo in the smaller active ports when the tide is out. This state of affairs can no longer be accepted for the giant ocean traders for whom enclosed dock systems or deep tidal berths are essential.

Many small ports recently 'retired' from commercial trade have of necessity been forced to find revenue from leisure activities such as yacht marinas, quayside property developments, and a scaled down fishing industry. Another once important coastal traffic around the United Kingdom was that of the regular passenger / cargo trade. This died out around 1960 as aviation and the motorways improved. Only where there are essential services to offshore islands, or where local ferry crossings can avoid long detours, are passenger services still maintained. Cross-Channel passenger and freight traffic is now almost entirely in the hands of the roll-on, roll-off giant ferries, again suitable only for berthing at major ports.

Our clockwise journey around the South West starts on the Dorset coast and progresses through South Devon and Cornwall to Lands End. Thence we proceed along the North Cornwall, and Devon coasts finally arriving in Somerset's Bridgwater Bay area. It has been impossible within the scope of this book to visit every place once considered a commercial port, but it is hoped that at least a 'flavour' of the area's shipping, harbours and trades has been realised. Some general and local maps are interspersed to aid the reader's navigation.

General Map No.1   Purbeck to River Exe

DORSET

DORCHESTER

Chesil Beach

Weymouth

Portland Harbour

Bill of Portland

Lulworth Cove

Wareham

Isle of Purbeck

St. Albans Head

Poole

BOURNEMOUTH

Swanage

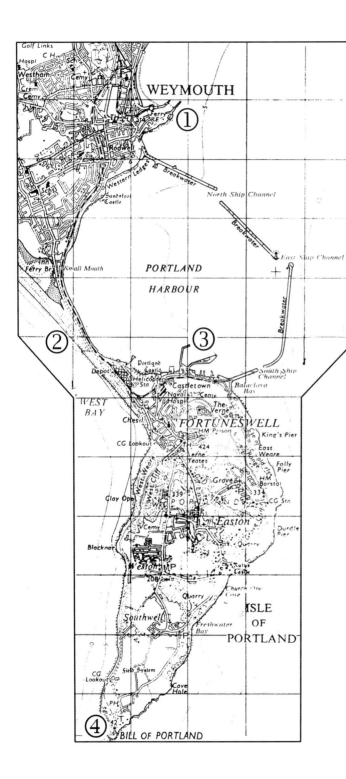

Local Map No.1
Weymouth and
Portland
(1)   Weymouth Harbour
(2)   Eastern end of
        Chesil Bank
(3)   Portland Port
(4)   Portland Lighthouses

1.   PS EMPRESS at Lulworth Cove →

The excursion trade developed rapidly with the advent of steam power. Railways and paddle steamers could offer hitherto impossible destinations to a previously 'static' population. Cosens of Weymouth were quick to establish themselves in 1845 for just this purpose and until their demise in 1967, operated no other type of vessel. In this tranquil 1930s setting, the iron hulled PS *Empress* 173g/1879 has gently pushed her bow to the shelving beach enabling passenger access ashore via a traditional stout, wheeled gangway. Close observation reveals a 'hauling-off' wire on her port quarter to assist departure. Iron hulled ships often had great longevity and *Empress* survived until 1955 as an active member of Cosens' fleet in the Bournemouth-Swanage- Weymouth-Portland locality. Her old fashioned oscillating engines were almost obsolete when installed, yet they served her well for seventy six years. The twin cylinders were situated below the line of the paddle shaft and swayed to and fro as the cranks revolved, there being no connecting rods. Boiler pressure was a mere 30 psi. Such was their uniqueness that upon demolition of the ship her engines were presented to the Southampton Maritime Museum.

2.   Weymouth in the 1900s ↓

Weymouth Port dates back to Roman times and a 'charter' in 1252 described it as a 'freeport and borough'. A further charter in 1571 Elizabethan times united it with Melcombe Regis, a settlement on the north side. Trade included wine, sugar and timber and from construction of the first rudimentary pier in 1618, the port steadily grew in importance. Railway access directly onto the quayside in the 1850s saw much improved handling facilities for passengers and freight, and by post WWI some six ships could be berthed. The Channel Island traffic became the staple trade together with the excursion business, however other cargoes declined as nearby Poole developed. Today, high speed ferries operate to the Channel Islands. In this early 1900s scene, a pair of paddlers lay at the pier, whilst opposite two splendid gaff-rigged schooners and a Victorian steam yacht, sit at their moorings. The cleanliness of sails indicates private yacht ownership - no sail trading vessels ever kept their sails that white!

3. TSS ROEBUCK and MAY

The Great Western Railway Company ordered a new pair of steamers for their Channel Islands service in 1897 from a shipyard at Barrow in Furness. *Roebuck* 1,186g/1897 and a near identical sister ship *Reindeer* were twin screw, reciprocating engined vessels and although undoubtedly a great advance on previous tonnage, they still offered scant shelter to passengers above deck. In the 1900s photograph at Weymouth one of the pair awaits the day's passengers and departure time, whilst nearby the sailing barge *May* 46r/1893 drifts out to sea on the calm morning.

4. YXPILA and SS SAMBUR

This fine, white hulled Finnish schooner is seen here unloading Baltic timber in 1937. She was registered at Rauma and built as recently as 1920. Encouraged by the abundant supplies of local timber, several Scandinavian and Baltic countries continued to construct wooden hulled cargo vessels right up to WWII. *Yxpila* was of 635 tons measurement, and probably of not inconsiderable auxiliary motor power. The Railway steamer on the right is one of a pair built in 1925 named *Sambur* and *Roebuck* (2), each of 776 gross tons, for the Channel Islands cargo service.

5. SS SUFFOLK COAST

Coast Lines ran a very comprehensive freight and passenger service around the UK coast for many decades, having absorbed many smaller firms along the way to consolidate operations. Goods of all types were handled from small consignments to complete cargoes. In this 1930s scene at Weymouth's Custom House Quay, the *Suffolk Coast* 870g/1917 has derricks rigged for cargo work whilst raising steam for the next leg of the voyage. Beyond lies yet another timber carrier in the form of a schooner, but seemingly steel hulled in construction. Today these quays mostly witness the local fishing fleet boats.

6. SS ST. JULIAN

This vessel and sister ship *St.Helier* both 1,885g/1925 were turbine powered steamers built at Glasgow as replacements for the 1897 pair described in No.3. Their design is markedly more modern in appearance as would be expected and yet open side alleyways are still present beneath the bridge area. With 4,350 ihp engines, speed achieved was in the order of 18 kts, quite some advance over their 1897 built reciprocating engined predecessors.

7. SS ST. PATRICK
This turbine powered ferry 3,482g/1948 is seen during one of her summer sojourns at Weymouth, providing additional capacity on the Channel Islands route. She was built for the Fishguard and Rosslare Railways and Harbours Company, but in effect was under British Railways control (British Transport Commission).The 1950s scene at Weymouth shows the large number of travelling electric cranes then in use on the quayside. *St.Patrick* illustrates clearly the increasing size of ferries and she had capacity for 1,300 passengers and 50 cars. A speed of 21kts could be achieved from her four steam turbines.

8. EARL OF PEMBROKE and KASKELOT
The Weymouth scene in July 2007, and gone are the traditional ferries. Moored in their place are two of Square Sail's barque rigged sailing ships. Normally based in Cornwall (see No.45), they are much employed by the film industry when traditionally rigged craft are required for authenticity. The white ferry terminal building now houses Condor Ferries' fast Channel Islands operations. Nearby an ex-Royal Navy fleet tender lies moored.

9. MV CONDOR VITESSE

Today's Weymouth-Channel Islands connection is maintained by high speed craft of the 'Incat' type. Freight traffic now largely moves by roll-on, roll-off ferries from Portsmouth, plus small containership. The Weymouth service now depends mostly on excursion passenger traffic plus cars. *Condor Vitesse* (seen here at Poole in 2004) can achieve speeds up to 39 kts given moderate seas. She is of 5,005grt and was built in 1997 to a design known as a 'wave piercing catamaran'. Continuing pressure from airlines and the increase in size of ferries operating elsewhere, thus precluding their use at Weymouth, has somewhat restricted operations here.

10. ST PORTWEY

Seen underway in splendid condition is the steam tug *Portwey* 94g/1927. She came to the area new under the ownership of the Weymouth and Portland Coaling Company - a title that precisely described operations involved - the bunkering of coal fired ships of all kinds. As oil firing of boilers superceded coal, *Portwey* moved down the coast to Falmouth where she continued to handle towage duties until retirement from trade. She escaped the breakers torch and is now active in the 'preservation' scene.

11. Portland from Weymouth

Although quarried for centuries beforehand, Portland stone grew more popular for the construction of great public buildings in the 1700s. Its special carving qualities and nearby access to seaborne transport for onward carriage made it eminently suitable. When the railway arrived in 1865 the heyday of quarrying had already passed, although the railway took its share of the remaining traffic at sea transport's loss. From the 1930s large flat-bed lorries came into use thereby ending the need for double handling of the stone, and the railway closed completely in 1965. From 1826 to 1930 an inclined plane wagon track, gravity worked, operated from the high level Priory Corner down to Castletown Pier for ship loading. Stone was brought from the outlying quarries by, at first horse, then steam drawn wagons. Portland has of course been well known as a Naval Port and the massive stone breakwaters were constructed between 1849 and 1903. The capacious harbour thus formed within would see up to a couple of hundred ships at anchor on occasion, and it became the Navy's principle sea training base. Today it is still visited by Naval vessels but since 1996 has developed into a servicing facility for passing merchant ships, its deepwater location being ideal.

The 2007 photograph taken from Weymouth's Fort Nothe shows two large vessels receiving attention in the anchorage.

12. Mulberry Harbour units

This view is roughly the reverse of No.11, the large tanker *Maria Tsakos* 57,925g/1998 in the anchorage, shows both direction and the immense size of the area encompassed by the port. The jetty for small motor boats in the foreground handles a service to Weymouth. Long gone are the paddle steamers that ranged far along what is now known as the 'Jurassic Coast'. Beyond the little jetty lay two remnants of the many scores of concrete caissons built during WWII.

They were towed across to the beaches of Normandy for the landings, sunk to provide an 'instant' harbour for onward movement of military equipment to the front - remarkable survivors indeed. Their importance in the assembly of the Mulberry Harbour was paramount. The Union flag flying just here seems singularly appropriate, in this July 2007 photograph.

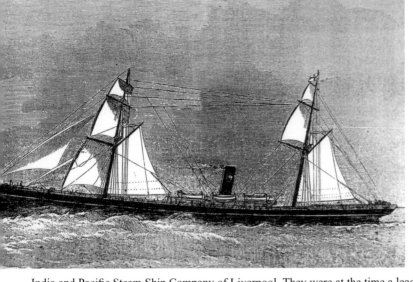

13. SS HAYTIAN (1875)

At first glance this fine old ship may appear not to have been destined for any particular association with Portland at all, however by the end of this description together with No.14, all will become clear. *Haytian* 2,350g/1875 was built for the then thriving West India and Pacific Steam Ship Company of Liverpool. They were at the time a leading player in trade to that part of the world with a fleet of a dozen or so steamers. Goods bound for the West Coast of North America were trans-shipped by rail across the Isthmus of Panama for onward shipment by sea. This was long before the advent of the Panama Canal. Work began on that mammoth engineering project in 1881, but it did not open to shipping until 1914. Returning to the *Haytian*, she represents an age when steam engines and boilers were becoming ever more efficient, yet ship owners were reluctant to totally dispense with sail. Coal bunkers took up valuable storage space thus reducing cargo capacity, and this ship's 'brig-like' sailing rig would have been most beneficial with favourable winds. The dreaded doldrums- areas of little or no wind were now no obstacle to regular trade. In due course *Haytian* was superceded by more modern tonnage and found her way to Portland Harbour for employment as a coal hulk described next. The image has been partially redrawn from a much faded line drawing.

14. Coal hulk HAYTIAN (to 1937)

Minus funnel, yards, and doubtless many other previously vital bits of equipment, the old ship has been cut down to coal hulk (storage) duty. Up until the 1930s many such vessels were placed strategically in hundreds of locations worldwide to enable merchant and naval coal fired ships to prosecute their voyages. A whole armada of coal carrying tramp steamers would maintain stocks as required, wherever. During her second career

at Portland, *Haytian* had the misfortune to be hit by a battleship in 1912, and the final indignity of being rammed by a torpedo boat in 1937. The photograph from that year shows the old ship settled by the stern, yet with those two lofty masts still pointing defiantly skywards. With the growth in the oil firing of boilers and subsequent motor powered ships, the necessity for such grimy edifices vanished by around WWII. Not, one would suspect, greatly missed by those who had to slave aboard them.

15. Portland Lighthouse

The first proper lighthouse built hereabouts dated from 1716 and consisted of a coal fired light. Now part of a tourist cottage complex, it is known as the 'Old Higher Light'. A second structure, the 'Lower Light', is now a bird observatory. The present working light tower dates from 1906 and opens to the Public. It rises some 43M (141ft) above sea level and is visible for 25 miles, exhibiting a white group flash (4) light every 20 secs. In the photograph the jagged nature of the rock shoreline is clearly apparent. Rock extraction began from such sites before the development of the inland quarries. Simple wooden derricks would load stone blocks into small coasting vessels when suitable fair weather and tidal restrictions allowed. Some small derricks were later used to launch local fishing boats. The waters around Portland's southern tip can be dangerous in all kinds of conditions. The legendary Portland 'race'- a powerful tidal stream, especially at spring tides when wind and tide direction conflict, has claimed many craft over the years.

16. TSS ROEBUCK at St. Helier, Jersey

Since the Channel Islands have been served for so long from Weymouth and the fact that they lay some 60 to 80 miles south of Portland allows us to make a brief diversion at this point. This image shows *Roebuck* already described in No.3 arriving from Weymouth at her destination of St. Helier. The journey cross Channel, especially in adverse winter weather would not be an easy one, since all shipping bound up and down Channel needed to be crossed at right angles to the course line. Also the waters surrounding the Channel Islands are littered with rocks fully or part submerged, with fast running tidal streams an additional hazard.

17. SS CAESAREA at St.Peter Port, Guernsey

The next three previously unpublished images from original large glass negatives date from the 1908-10 period, and are included to illustrate how cargo and passenger handling has changed in the last century. In this scene the London and South Western Railway Company (rival to the Great Western) steamer *Caesarea* 1,505g/1910, a three turbine powered vessel is berthed at St.Peter Port. The clarity of detail in the photo is amazing and close examination reveals great piles of empty wicker produce baskets, several horse drawn carts and vans, one very early motor vehicle, electric quayside cranes and a seemingly non-wired telegraph pole. The two Fuzzey Company antique vans are interesting, as they represent that early form of 'through containerisation' suited to road or rail use. The lifting straps can be clearly seen. One crane is busily working the ship's hold. *Caesarea* has an enormous old fashioned bow anchor poised overside ready for letting go if so required, in those difficult confined waters nearby. The open navigation bridge has been given the customary extra wind and spray protection by way of a white canvas dodger.

18. St. Peter Port around 1910

This similarly dated image shows sailing time drawing near. A large number of folk appear just about everywhere, and one is hard pressed to find anyone without a hat! The group on the quayside are sending parcels onboard by way of a sliding ramp, supervised by a junior officer. Lying between the crane rails is a horse lifting crate with wire slings. Upon the upper deck, first class passengers survey the scene- some additional rather miniscule shelters have been provided by the mast base for their general well being en route. The whole makes an interesting comparison to the rather clinical drive-on, drive-off procedures of today!

19. 'Produce to load'

Passengers are filing aboard an unidentified L&SWR steamer here at St.Peter Port. This ship will be on the rival Southampton service and a part consignment of Island produce awaits loading whilst be-capped ships' officers jolly things along. A hand cart in the foreground is laden with rope lifting strops ready for any eventuality. Everything visible suggests the need for much manpower and perhaps the produce awaits the next cargo steamer due.

20. SS NERMA at West Bay

Returning to the Mainland we see here the Danish steamer *Nerma* 752g/950d/ 1893 at West Bay harbour, Bridport. Rigged with cargo gaffs and tackle she is believed to have brought a cargo of jute from the Latvian port of Riga for use in West Bay's once busy ropemaking works. The image dates from the early 1900s and the uncluttered countryside beyond is worthy of note - the only building visible is still there today - the ancient salt-house. *Nerma's* owners have also stood the test of time, J.Lauritzen & Co. of Esbjerg are today very much involved in ocean trading with much larger ships. The *Nerma* passed to another Danish owner, Marius Nielsen in 1916, but would sadly succumb to a German submarine torpedo, not far away off Berry Head in 1917. She was voyaging from St.Malo to Port Talbot in ballast when hit, and some survivors were duly landed at Torquay.

21. LEONARD PIPER

Bridport's delightful little harbour at West Bay came into existence long ago. Attempts were made as early as 1400 to establish a port at the mouth of the River Britt which had been spasmodically navigable by small vessels. As with many other minor English Channel ports, storm damage (repeated), littoral shingle drift (permanent), and river silting (regular), all conspired to hinder progress. By the close of the eighteenth century a greater degree of stabilisation had been achieved, and trade flourished, together with wooden ship building and rope making. Later imports consisted of coal (domestic and gasworks), timber and fertilisers. Return cargoes for the ships mainly consisted of 'gravel' won from the local beaches. With the increase in ship sizes, visits by commercial vessels had tapered off to a mere 16 in 1983, handling just 5,811 tons of cargo. By around 1987 ships had simply outgrown West Bay's capacity for 300 tonners, and cargo operations ceased. In the 1930s scene, the sailing barge *Leonard Piper* 99r/1910 awaits a gravel cargo. She has already been fitted with an auxiliary motor, since the mizzen mast has been removed, and a small wheelhouse built in lieu. Beyond can be seen the masts of a ketch, and across the dock one of Swedish Lloyd's early small tramp steamers is in port. She would probably have brought jute or a cargo of Baltic timber, and their distinctive funnel marking clearly shows. The long boardwalk upon which the photographer stood enabled gangs of men to lead in the bow ropes of visiting non-powered ships. The sluice gates from the River Britt are visible beyond.

22. Harbour reconstruction, West Bay

In this 2004 photograph much work is underway evidenced by workboats and a small construction rig beyond. A brand new outer breakwater angled out from the Western shore nears completion, and now bars the old view of the sea from this point. The boardwalk described in No.21 has now gone, and further work within the new areas created involves provision of facilities for visiting yachts. The smart little tug *Wilanne*, Dutch built, belongs to Williams Shipping of Southampton. The imposing block beyond the cars was built as long ago as 1885, when

the Great Western Railway had hoped to develop West Bay's tourism, sadly, no such thing occurred and passenger trains ceased south of Bridport town in 1930.

23. New breakwaters

This view actually pre-dates No.22 and shows progress underway in 2003 on the angled outer breakwater. The narrow entrance between the two old short piers is however still clearly intact. One large vessel has called since the alterations when in 2006, MV *Balmoral* made a visit. It would appear that in this new century, leisure facilities and new homes have finally achieved what the GWR once set out to do. Of course there is one major difference today - road traffic domination!

24. The Cobb, Lyme Regis

Lyme was recorded as a port in 1250 and its ancient breakwater, known as The Cobb has variously been extended and reconstructed over the centuries. Local commercial shipping traffic, once quite prolific, dwindled during the inter war years to a mere 13 ships by 1938. The port was closed during WWII, and this proved terminal as no revival in cargo operations occurred. In the 1900s view an assortment of schooners and ketches are moored in the harbour along with a modest number of local fishing boats and small craft.

25. MV VELOCITAS at Lyme Regis

Arriving with 86 standards of sawn Baltic timber is the little Dutch coaster *Velocitas* 199g/1936. Registered at Groningen, she is representative of literally hundreds of vessels, similar in size and layout. They could carry some 250 tons of whatever was on offer anywhere around the North Sea, British Isles, English Channel and Baltic Sea areas. Frequently family owned and run - the master was often the owner and his wife and other family members made up the crew.

Washing appears on the line above the after derrick. Within a couple of years of this image, no further cargoes would arrive, and centuries of trade thus ended here.

26. Low tide at Lyme

In this 2006 scene, small inshore fishing boats and yachts rest at low water. A major civil engineering project is underway right around the bay to build up beaches and construct substantial retaining walls. This work will ensure stability for Lyme's unstable ground, and thus secure its fine resort status for decades to come.

27. MV DIET at Exmouth Dock

The River Exe estuary has been of strategic and commercial importance for perhaps two millennia. In 1864 the Exmouth Dock Company built a 570ft by 270ft basin for commercial shipping. In 1891 the Company's title was altered to reflect their growing involvement in the paddle steamer excursion trade, then booming. The dock could handle several cargo ships of up to about 750 tons capacity, involved in the coal, timber, fertiliser, grain, woodpulp and esparto grass trades – the latter two being vital ingredients in the paper manufacturing industry. Sand and ballast were also landed. The Dock closed to trade in 1990 with the remaining cargoes shifting across to Teignmouth. Imports of coal for the local gasworks had ceased in 1971 when the nation's North Sea gas pipeline network reached these parts, superceding local generation. In the photograph from around 1970, two coasters are working cargo in the Dock and the nearest MV *Diet* 397g/1940 begins to reflect the growing size of such vessels - her carrying capacity was about 500 tons.

28. MV OSTARA

Seen here entering Exmouth Dock is another Dutchman, the *Ostara* 422g/1957. Just visible beyond is one of South Coast Shipping's sand dredgers, evidenced by the distinctive black diamond on a white banded funnel. They were at the time part of the Cory Group. By this time radar had been fitted to most coasters, regulations so requiring it to be.

29. MV SAND SNIPE

The possible owner of the funnel visible in No.28, here we see the *Sand Snipe* 517g/1961 returning from the dredging grounds with a full load of sand or ballast for the building trade. The last of the water is draining from the hold via the ship's scuppers, and the long suction dredging pipe fitted to the ship's starboard side lies secured below its handling davits. The ship was probably new in this photo as she had yet to be fitted with radar. The

additional light fittings on the foremast are the all-round signals to indicate 'engaged in under water operations' ie, dredging at night.

30. Exmouth Dock entrance in 2006

This image makes an interesting comparison to the trading days of No.28. Designer homes now 'grace' the quayside around the dock which has become a marina. A new lifting type bascule bridge has appeared across the entrance channel, and local fishing vessels land their catch in the foreground. Extensive piling and regeneration is underway on the left bank.

Local Map No. 2   Exe Estuary

(1)   Exeter City Dock
(2)   Exeter Ship Canal
(3)   Turf Lock
(4)   Topsham Quays

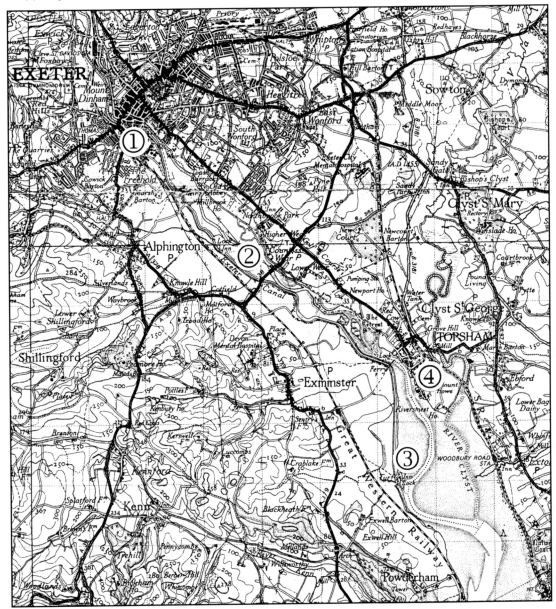

31. BUTTERCUP at Topsham ⭦

A small quay is known to have existed at Topsham in the early 1300s and because of deeper water in this part of the Exe estuary, shipbuilding duly became established. The construction of a weir above Topsham by the Earl and Countess of Devon precluded direct trade to Exeter, thus enhancing Topsham's position in the 1400s. In common with many previously isolated places, arrival of the railway brought direct access and improved quaysides in the 1860s. Wooden ship building, long in the hands of the Holman family, declined from the 1870s as wooden hulls lost out to iron then steel types, constructed elsewhere. Ship repair work and boat building remained and trade in stone, coal, fertilisers and large items continued coastwise. Post WWII an import terminal for the well known Danish Tuborg Lager Company was established and grain, flour, timber and building materials continued to be handled. Latterly the quay accepted ships up to around 600 tons capacity, but by 1985 commercial shipping ceased to visit. In the scene from around 1900 the ketch *Buttercup*, owned at Exeter is in drydock for repairs, well shored up with traditional baulks of timber.

32. A schooner at Topsham ⭧

In this photograph dating from around 1909, a three masted schooner has been unloading at the wharf. Beyond, out in the river a local ketch with a very tall topmast sits awaiting her next turn of duty, whilst further over, another local trader is looking very 'down at heel', possibly no longer active. Vessels such as these three were the backbone of coastal trading for the previous couple of centuries, or more.

← 33. MV C. HERUP

Built at Marstal, Denmark where many wooden sailing cargo vessels had come off the slipways, this smart little motor coaster became a regular to Topsham for many years. At a mere 197g/1957 built, she was affectionately known as the 'Tuborg Lager boat'. Everything about the ship is robust and workmanlike. On deck may be seen a few of the larger cylindrical type lager tanks, well lashed down for the North Sea-English Channel passage, as indeed they needed to be!

← 34. Topsham Quay in 2006

The stone faced, concrete apron quay was Topsham's final berth for commercial vessels, and post WWII some 5,000 tons of cargo per month were handled. The large brick built warehouse became the Tuborg lager depot. Today it is open to the public as an antique and collectors' establishment. The shallow nature of the Exe is plain to see as a variety of craft sitting on the bottom well illustrate, Topsham's final trade moved down to Exmouth Dock upon the wharf's closure.

35. MV IRIS at Exeter Dock

Given a decent rise of tide, small craft had managed to reach Exeter City on the River Exe, from Roman times. The weir already mentioned in No.31 (Countess Wear), precluded further waterborne traffic to the City. In the 1560s a small canal permitted tiny barges to reach quays in the heart of Exeter, but this still relied upon good tides downstream, and good river flow from upstream, for barge movement. Around 1700 the canal was much deepened over about three miles and later still extended a further two miles down the estuary to Turf Lock. By 1820, ships of 9ft draught were transitting the canal, later increased to 14 ft navigation would however always be limited by lock dimensions, and finally the limits were for ships not exceeding 122ft by 26ft, length and breadth. In its latter years of operation 10ft 06in was regarded as the safe working draught, equating to a ship's carrying capacity of some 350 tons. Coal imports ceased when local gas generation closed down and the small petroleum depot followed in 1973. The last 'regular' ship was the Water Authority's MT *Countess Wear* 245g/1963 which carried material for dumping at sea, until legislation banned such practices. In the 1950s photograph Baltic timber is stacked on the quayside after discharge from the Dutch coaster Iris 200g/250d/1937. As we have already seen, such vessels carried a great tonnage of cargo to minor English ports from the 1920s to the 1960s.

36. MT ESSO JERSEY

Specially built to access Turf Lock and deliver petroleum products to Exeter, *Esso Jersey* 313g/350d/1962 would probably have been named '*Esso Exeter*' had it not been for the fact that a large ocean going tanker already had that name. The photograph from the early 1960s shows this smart little ship laden and heading westwards down the Solent, having just departed Fawley and rounded Calshot Spit. Careful examination of the background reveals one of the legendary Princess flying boats which sadly spent no time in the air but years in lay-up, mothballed for a future which never came.

37. Exeter City Dock

The 2006 photograph shows a variety of non-commercial craft based in the once busy dock. This view is from the Kings Arm Sluice end which effectively marks the end of the Ship Canal from Turf Lock. The main flow of the River Exe passes by to the right of the boats perched up on the wall.

General Map No.2   River Exe to River Tamar

38. MV AAR at Teignmouth

Teignmouth as a port was not mentioned in the Domesday Book, yet fishing and trade appear to have flourished in the Middle Ages. In the 1700s in common with a number of West Country ports, trade with Newfoundland was considerable. By the 1820s granite from Haytor quarries became a major coastwise traffic. In 1853 some 40,000 tons of coal and culm were imported whilst 80,000 tons of clay along with some iron, lead and manganese went outwards. In 1938 the Teignmouth Quay Company oversaw improvements which would allow 1,000 ton ships to berth with a 14ft draught, tide permitting. Local ball clay from the Bovey Tracey workings became the major export, whilst coal, timber and woodpulp for the Culm Valley Paper Factory were major imports. By 1985 further dredging and quay improvements permitted ships in the 2,000 to 3,000 ton range to berth on suitable tides. The 1937 photograph shows the West German motor schooner *Aar* 330g/1932 moored at the quay. She had brought Baltic timber and doubtless left with an export clay cargo. Built at Brake by C.Luhring to an 'old' design, she was basically a modern motorship, yet a set of auxiliary sails would be used to great benefit when conditions allowed.

39. MV BREEWIJD

Spout loading of ball clay is underway into the after hold of the Dutch *Breewijd* 494g/1965 in this late 1960s image. Beyond, on the end dock, lies another similar sized coaster, the *Carpe Diem* of Stockevik, Sweden. In the early 1960s some 200,000 tons of ball (china) clay were annually exported, whilst coal and timber were the main inbound commodities.

40. MV WARFLETH

In this 2007 scene the German operated *Warfleth* 1,022g/1980 is sailing on completion of loading. She is an early version of the L.A.D. (low air draught) type with retractable wheelhouse suited to transitting the River Rhine and Europe's inland waterway system. Masts are similarly hinged to give the necessary clearance. With a cargo capacity of just over 1,000 tons, such small ships are becoming something of a rarity today, in that never ending search for economy of scale in operation. RMS on the ship's side stands for the line, 'Rhein-Maas-See'.

41. MV CASABLANCA

Seen arriving to load at Teignmouth in May 2007 is a larger German operated ship, the *Casablanca* 2,061g/3,002d/1994. She represents a major size increase in the type just described in No.40. In common with current world practices this ship is registered 'offshore' in St. Johns, Antigua and Barbuda, in the Carribean. Also visible on the poop deck bulwark is her official International Maritime Authority (IMO) number, now required to be shown by all international trading vessels. In recent years up to 1,000 ships per year, and on occasion 5,000 tons of ball clay, have been loaded in one day at Teignmouth, all from the Bovey Tracey workings. The smart little Teignmouth to Shaldon ferry waits for a clear run to the other side of the Teign with just two passengers this trip.

Local Map No.3   Tor Bay

(1)   Torquay Harbour
(2)   Brixham Harbour

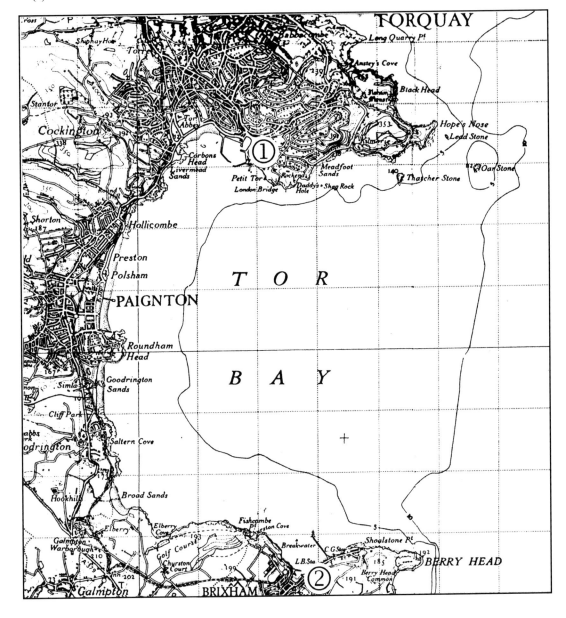

42. Coal unloading at Torquay

This delightful pre-1900 image shows a small coastal steamer of just a few hundred tons unloading coal to the shore bunkers just visible on the right. The method employed is time honoured. From booms aloft, gin tackles will raise baskets of coal from the holds by manpower, to be emptied into large wheelbarrows. These will be pushed ashore via gangplanks. An extra large cart-width gangway is visible on the quay for use when tide height so permits access. The old ship, gently letting off steam, still carries sails seen brailed to the masts, and the forecastle head is of the old 'whaleback' type. She probably dates from the 1860s. Torquay had a not inconsiderable coastal trade, and much coal would have been brought in for domestic, industrial and gas works use. A three masted schooner can be seen in the inner basin.

43. SS LA DUCHESSE DE BRETAGNE

At the end of her career on the Newhaven-Dieppe railway ferry service, new horizons beckoned for the old SS *Brighton* 2,875g/1950. Roll-on, roll-off ferries had rendered this passenger only vessel redundant on the route, and her construction was such as to preclude full conversion. So she moved down Channel to the Torbay area to be run as an excursion ferry for Jersey Shipping to the Channel Islands and St.Malo. In the photograph from around 1967 the ship looks smart with a new funnel logo, but otherwise little altered from her Newhaven days. Some provision has been made for cars on the extended upper deck, aft. Always a fast vessel, her steam turbines could muster over 24kts but oil fired boilers would have been very thirsty, and none too economical for her owners.

44. MV FRIARS CRAIG

Motor coasters continued to be owned in small ports around the coast in some numbers until two or three decades ago. Here we see the little *Friars Craig* 590g/1938 laden, at sea. By the early 1970s she was running for G.Dupenois of Torquay, having previously been named *Salcombe* until 1969, and *Camroux IV* until 1942.

45. CORNISH BELLE

Local excursions continue to thrive around the holiday area of Torbay, and here the wooden hulled *Cornish Belle* is setting off towards Paignton and Brixham. It was a chilly April day in 2007 and passenger numbers seem to reflect that fact. The little vessel has evidently been much cared for and modernised – wooden hulled craft of this type are not so common now. The tall masts inside the Torquay breakwater belong to the ketch yacht *Queen Galadriel*, an ex Baltic trader.

46. TORBAY BELLE

Another Torquay excursion vessel awaits warmer days for a full load of passengers. This ship started life as a ferry in Scotland, and came South in recent years to join the local fleet. Some modifications to the accommodation have been made to this steel hulled vessel since her Scottish days as *Loch Awe* and *Lochmor*. The quay visible on the left by the concrete slipway is approximately where much coal heaving took place a century earlier, as witnessed in No.42.

47. JANE WHEATON at Brixham

An atmospheric scene in Brixham Harbour probably around 1890 and the Rye, Sussex built topsail schooner *Jane Wheaton* 185g/1863 is awaiting a rise of tide. She is flanked by a couple of Brixham's legendary sailing trawlers the nearest of which shows Dartmouth registration lettering. The well known 'BM' code for Brixham fishing vessels did not appear until 1902.

48. SS FORDHAM

Despite its major pre-occupation with the fishing fleet, Brixham saw other types of visiting ships and here around 1922 the steam coaster *Fordham* 458g/1897 is moored in the harbour. She had been built at Ayr, by S. Macknight & Co. and at first sailed under the name of *Latchford*. Her owners in 1922 were the London Transport Company.

49. Brixham fishing fleet in 2007

The expanded modern harbour today homes a not inconsiderable fleet of fishing vessels ranging from small inshore types to more distant-water boats. With current rules and fishing quotas permitted, the industry is not enjoying the best of times. Brixham's other great significance has long been its importance as a ship's pilot boarding service provider. Ships requiring a Channel or North Sea Pilot inbound or to drop the pilot outbound, can do so in the sheltered lee of the bay, by the launches provided.

The Timber Trade

The sawn timber trade, particularly from the Baltic countries is an old one. Traditionally labour intensive in every aspect from the saw mills, to loading of the ships, and their ultimate discharge. Large gangs individually stowed battens, boards, deals and planks as tightly as possible in the ship's holds. Timber is a relatively light cargo, and in order to bring a ship down to her loadline marks, a deck cargo 'raft' had to be assembled on top of the loaded holds and closed hatches. Regulations evolved for the safe stowage, sea carriage and operation of such ships carrying timber, and provision had to be made for vertical timber stanchions, wire lashings and safety lines for the crew to move about the ship. On arrival at the discharge port equally large gangs of stevedores would descend upon the ship to set about extricating the timber stow, piece by piece. Timber measurement was a complex subject, there being a number of variations worldwide. A well known measure in the UK/North European trade was the 'Petrograd Standard'. This consisted of 120 pieces 1.5in. by 11in. by 12ft, equalling 165cu.ft. The term '100 deals' perversely implied 120 pieces. In recent decades there has been much standardisation in line with metrication, whereby 'plastic wrapped' and 'banded' packages are the norm. This makes for much greater ease of handling and few gaps in stowage onboard in the box shaped holds of modern vessels in the trade. In turn this reduces the size of additional deck cargo required to fully load the ships. In any case, timber importers had become less enthusiastic about salt water soaked deck cargo! For Baltic softwood, 1 standard roughly equated to 2.5 -3 tons in weight. A cubic metre of timber is also known as a 'stere'. Images 50 and 52 clearly highlight both old and new handling techniques.

50. ECKHOLM at Totnes

This sylvan scene belies the fact that much hard manual work is well underway. The date is around 1908 and the white, wooden hulled, gaff rigged Danish schooner *Eckholm*, has brought in a good load of Baltic timber. The gang is stacking the varying lengths upon the quayside, whilst the bowler hatted foreman stands behind the cart – all are definitely posing for their photograph. The ship is a typical Scandinavian schooner of her day, and most unlikely to have any form of propulsion other than the wind. The jib sails appear new and have been left aloft to dry in the light airs, whilst sunshine percolates through the trees on the end of Vire Island. The family business of F.J.Reeves & Co, began timber importing at Totnes, eleven miles upstream from Dartmouth, in 1900. The story continues in No.52.

Local Map No.4   River Dart

(1) Totnes wharves
(2) Noss Shipyard
(3) Kingswear
(4) Dartmouth Lower Ferry

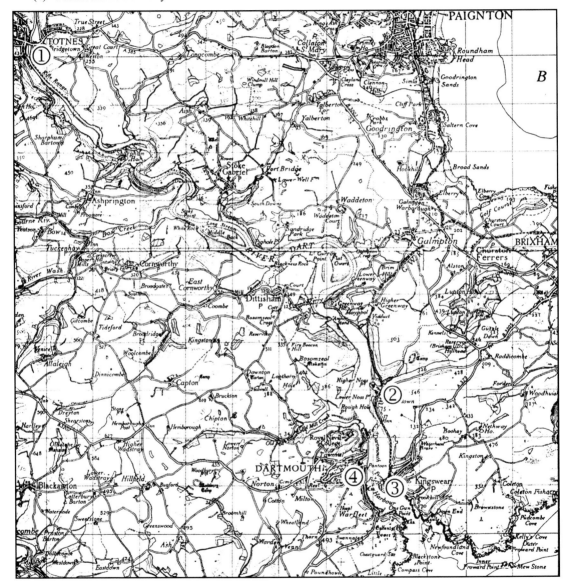

51. PS KINGSWEAR CASTLE

The image dates from the 1930s and shows Totnes landing stage on the East bank of the River Dart. The river paddle steamer *Kingswear Castle* 94g/1924 looks to be well laden with passengers for her run back down river to Dartmouth. This little ship was one of a small fleet and would, in the years to come have the good fortune to be fully restored for further service. Today she operates a full summer cruise programme on the River Medway, based at Chatham. Note the little building beyond the ship's mast – it will appear again.

52. MV ASTRID BRES

The Reeves Group continued to import timber at Totnes into the 1980s. An area of waste ground further down stream from the No.50 location enabled the new Baltic Wharf to be constructed, suitable with the aid of an enlarged turning area, to accept shiploads of around 1,000 tons apiece. In this image the Danish firm Nielsen & Bresling's vessel, *Astrid Bres* 499g/1977 is unloading neat packaged timber by ship's derrick. The flags flying and dignitaries on the quayside indicate that this was indeed a special arrival – that of the first larger shipment. The ship had been specially lengthened in 1981 to take advantage of the new facilities. Finally, ships up to 220ft in length with a draught of 12ft could be accommodated.

53. Totnes landing stage in 2007

Beyond the white yacht the little building mentioned in No.51 still stands some seventy years later. The clear waters of the Dart continue to flow by the present landing stage whilst, on the opposite bank the once busy Baltic Wharf has found new life after the cessation of shipping.

54. MV DART EXPLORER

On a cool May evening in 2007 any passengers onboard for the run down to Dartmouth appear to have opted for the internal accommodation. This fine, modern catamaran hulled, river cruiser seems light years away from the coal fired paddler *Kingswear Castle*. The twin hulls and beamy design makes an ideal viewing platform especially for shallow locations.

55. Dartmouth and the Royal Naval College

The well protected deepwater anchorage at Dartmouth was known to have been used as a port before 1049. In the fourteenth and fifteenth centuries trade flourished with Brittany and Bordeaux. In the last century or so, ships up to some 600ft in length have been able to moor to buoys in the river. The coal wharf at Kingswear could accommodate coasters up to about 250ft in length. In 1863 the old 'wooden-walls' warships *Britannia* and *Hindostan* were brought in to form the foundation of the famous Royal Naval College. The magnificent hilltop buildings of the shore based establishment date from 1905. Dartmouth's access to, and shelter from the sea, also saw the growth of the coal bunkering trade serving passing ships, as steam supplanted sail. A shipyard opened at Sandquay in 1800, and in 1861 George Philip founded the firm of Philip & Son, Ltd., Shipbuilders & Engineers. Over the ensuing 130 years they turned out almost 1,500 craft of many types for private, merchant and naval owners. The following list is far from complete but it helps illustrate the range involved:- schooners, ketches, cutters, yawls, steam tugs, paddlers, launches, cargo vessels, trawlers, drifters, ferries, lightships, barges, pilot cutters, tankers, yachts, mine layers, mine sweepers, corvettes, buoy tenders, boom defence vessels, armament carriers, air sea rescue launches, pinnaces, water carriers, motor tugs, motor coasters and motor fishing vessels. The firm sadly closed for business in 1999. In the scene from around 1930 numerous yachts, sail and steam are at anchor with one trading schooner. Beyond, the R.N. College buildings stand proudly upon the hill above the town. Far right can just be seen the floating dock lying off Philip & Son's Sandquay Yard. In recent years some cruise ships have visited Dartmouth's moorings.

56. River Dart 'lay-ups'

This view up-river continues across from No.55 with Sandquay middle left. The scene dates from the late 1920s and shows a good number of merchantmen in lay-up during the depression years which peaked around 1932. Just discernible further up the River Dart ships are moored in pairs, and it was not uncommon for twenty to thirty to be present, as all awaited better trading times. The motley group of craft middle right are members of the coal bunkering brigade. Two of Dartmouth's larger hulks were in fact cut down sailing ships, the *Dagny* 1,144r/1889 was an iron hulled, Liverpool registered barque; the *Sorknes* 1,525r/1893 had been a Cardiff registered steel barque. Their final employment as coaling hulks at Dartmouth was for the Channel Coaling Company. Oil firing of steam ship boilers saw the demise of the hulks by around WWII.

57. SS BOVEY TRACEY

Both Dartmouth and Torquay had coal bunkering operations run by the firm of Renwick, Wilton & Co. from the 1880s. A fleet of steam colliers brought the coal south from the Tyne and although the ships were sold off at the end of WWI, the Wilton part of the firm continued in the London coal trade until WWII. *Bovey Tracey* 1,212g/1930 was one of the very last 'midships' design type colliers, but she sadly succumbed as a war casualty on the East Coast in 1941.

58. SS LANCASHIRE

Seen being turned by a small tug off Dartmouth in the 1930s is the Bibby Line troopship *Lancashire* 10,391g/1917. The line operated a number of similar four masted liners and some were taken up by the Government as troop transports. These ships always carried a broad band painted around the hull. One or two of the class were totally rebuilt with motors replacing triple expansion engines, and just two masts to present a more modern appearance. Note the large number of lifeboats including additional foredeck sets. When Far-Eastern campaigns were less frenetic, Dartmouth would often be used as a seasonal lay-up location.

59. SS THE MEW

One of the Great Western Railway Company's less glamourous vessels was this fine old workhorse, *The Mew* 117g/1908. She spent decades running across the Dart from the Dartmouth waterfront to Kingswear Station. In early photographs the ship had a very tall spindly funnel, but by the time of this image a more modern 'squat' version has been installed, along with an 'improved' wheelhouse. Some provision was evidently made for wheeled traffic, as a rather grand looking limousine may be seen on the poop deck. Her stalwart service ended under British Railways' control in the 1950s.

60. To Kingswear Station

Suitably illustrating Dartmouth's sheltered location (this is the view towards the sea), we see one of F.T.Everard's 'yellow-peril' motor coasters unloading coal to both rail wagons and a barge, at Kingswear. This class of yellow hulled motor coaster entered service in the early 1950s. Far left, sitting on their moorings, a group of Dart excursion vessels, no less than three of which are paddlers, await action. On the far right a buoy tender vessel has just entered port.

61. MV LADY SYLVIA

This neat little motor ship and the subject of No.62 are included as fine examples of ships built by Philip & Son, of Dartmouth. *Lady Sylvia* 370g/1952 is very much designed along the lines of the Dutch coasters – the single mast is 'tabernacled' whereby it can be lowered for passage under bridges. This ship was one of a small fleet operated by Thomas Watson (Shipping) Ltd., of Rochester. Propulsion was by a Crossley oil engine.

62. MT ESSO BRIXHAM

A ship with a local name, The U.K. Esso Tanker fleet numbered 15-20 ships in the 1950s and this included true coastal vessels and a number of harbour 'bunkering' craft for fuel oil. The latter types had taken over the coal hulk role of earlier ship bunkering operations. Oil firing of boilers and diesel powered motorships now reigned supreme across the world's oceans. *Esso Brixham* 758g/1957 was capable of carrying around 1,000 tons of cargo, and was suited to both harbour and coastal work. She has been built with extra rubbing strakes, and evidently has a good supply of motor tyres for fendering against larger ships and dock walls.

63.   Dartmouth Castle & Dittisham Princess

Here off the Dartmouth waterfront in May 2007 are two examples of the modern local excursion fleet. *Dartmouth Castle* operates for Devon Princess Cruises, and the passing *Dittisham Princess* runs for River Link. Beyond lies moored the inevitable fuel barge now essential at marinas to keep the motor yachts running.

64.   Dartmouth Lower Ferry

Generations of 'pontoon' type ferries have operated on this particular crossing, powered by motor launch type tugs. The present floats have hydraulically powered end ramps and can accommodate 6-8 vehicles. Two *'Hauley'* tugs and their floats run together at busy times on this short crossing to Kingswear during which, they must contend with strong tidal streams and much boat traffic.

65. LORD DEVON at Salcombe

Our next port of call is Salcombe and the Kingsbridge Estuary. This inlet was another useful 'bolt-hole' for sailing vessels seeking shelter from the Channel gales. Many small ships could safely anchor within. Salcombe's prosperity grew especially when the local shipyard production was at its peak. Between 1796-1887 some 200 various size and type vessels were launched, regularly employing 200 men. Spars, masts, blocks, pumps, casks and 'trenails' were just some of the essential components also locally manufactured. In 1848 it was reported that cargo handled amounted to 16,273 tons including coal, timber, fruit and groceries. Ship losses at sea, as was the case more generally at the time were high, yet men always came forward to go to sea, and new ships were soon sent down the slipways. Today, much of the infrastructure of this delightful little town owes its existence to those mariners and ship builders and the prosperity they brought. 1879 was seen locally as the death knell for local shipyards, as steam ships and steel hulls were built elsewhere. Fishing and small boat construction continued. In this fine image the last sailing ship built for the Salcombe Ship Owning Company is seen awaiting the tide off Folly Quay. *Lord Devon* 114r/1885 was a topsail schooner.

66. Salcombe waterfront in 2007

Small craft abound today in this tranquil scene with the main estuary winding its way up to Kingsbridge in the far right distance.

67. PS SALCOMBE CASTLE

With Kingsbridge Church tower dead centre, this photograph dates from the early 1900s. Philip & Son of Dartmouth built this tiny paddle steamer in 1897 for the service between Salcombe and Kingsbridge. At a mere 34grt she is seen here arriving at Kingsbridge and a couple of local boats seem to have the benefit of a tow. The little ship's dimensions were just 61ft loa and 12ft beam, (this latter figure would be doubled over the paddle boxes). The steam engine was rated at 15hp. After WWI she returned briefly to her old route, but was broken up at Salcombe in 1920 after a very brief career, for a paddle steamer. The boy on horseback seems more interested in the photographer than the arrival of the steamer.

← 68. EFFORT & SS KINGSBRIDGE PACKET

Kingsbridge similarly had a ship building heyday and between 1837 and closure in the early 1900s, no less than 86 ships were launched. Two ropeworks and an iron foundry provided their necessary components. In 1893, the Great Western Railway Company's branch line arrived, yet despite bringing more people and goods in, coal, timber and building materials continued to be shipped up the estuary from Salcombe. The busy scene from around 1900 shows four vessels alongside. Nearest is the ketch *Effort* 85r/1880 and locally built. Next in line is the topsail schooner *Moss Rose*, then the steamer *Kingsbridge Packet* 111g/1879, she was the local 'supply' ship owned by W.H.Prowse of Salcombe. Of iron construction, she came from Harvey's Yard at Hayle in Cornwall. Three different *Kingsbridge Packets* are believed to have operated on the Plymouth-Salcombe-Kingsbridge service between 1857 and the 1900s. The furthest vessel appears to be a schooner under repair.

69. Kingsbridge Quay in 2007

The boy on the horse about one hundred years ago in No.67 would have been standing about where the person is walking along the quay. The shallow nature of the waterway here today provides moorings strictly for the lighter kind of boat.

Plymouth

The port was certainly well established in 1311 and by Queen Elizabeth I reign was deemed to be one of England's foremost. In the early 1700s the sugar importing and refining industry began and there was much trade with Virginia and the West Indies. Within the bounds of the Sound apart from the Naval presence at Devonport, there were several distinct trading areas, namely:- The River Plym, Cattewater, Sutton Harbour, Millbay and Stonehouse. Also, the many creeks and rivers leading off the River Tamar saw much waterborne traffic to now long forgotten wharves, all contributing to the overall industrial activity within the port. The mighty stone breakwater constructed from 1812-1840 gave protection to all shipping within the Sound from on-shore gales and heavy seas. The Great Western Railway Company came to own and develop the most important docks, and Millbay Pier handled passengers and mails from liners visiting out in the Sound. In the 1930s the largest ocean cargo ships could be handled and grain, fruit and general cargoes were important. Trinity Pier also handled general goods and continental traffic. The Railway Company also operated a commercial drydock. By the 1960s Cattewater Harbour was run as a separate entity by its Commissioners, and Millbay Docks by British Transport. Coast Lines' intensive UK coastal passenger and freight services ran from Victoria Wharves. Today, Sutton Harbour is the base for fishing vessels – this had been an earlier commercial hub. Mail ships ceased to call in 1963 when the long distance overseas post moved to the aviation network. Local trading vessels carried cargoes generated by quarrying, mining, brickmaking, farming and market gardening. Now the principle cargo wharves are at Cattedown and Victoria Wharves. The outer part of the Millbay Docks has been developed as the roll-on, roll-off cross Channel ferry terminal.

70. SS LADY GWENDOLEN

Arriving at Plymouth around 1912 is the British & Irish Steamship Company's *Lady Gwendolen* 2,163g/1911. She was one of a fleet of coastwise passenger / cargo steamers which connected various major ports and cities around the British Isles. Rates would generally be a good deal cheaper than train fares and, weather permitting, passages quite speedy. This ship has a completely open bridge with chart room below, and evidently considerable passenger accommodation, judging by the rows of portholes. A small staysail is furled ready for action above the forecastle head, and would probably help in turning the vessel off the berth, given a bit of a breeze – bow thrusters had definitely not yet arrived. The sender of this card reported, "a rather rough afternoon, but no one was ill!"

71. SS NEW VERDUN

The Plymouth, Channel Islands and Brittany Steam Ship Co. Ltd., of Plymouth, ran small vessels on the trade routes well described by their title. *New Verdun* 332g/1907 ran until the firm was taken over by the Coast Lines Group in 1937. Originally this little steamer's name had simply been *Verdun*, She was built in Marstal, Denmark and came to Plymouth registry in 1926. The extended saloon on the poop deck shows that a few passengers could be carried if necessary. The small wheelhouse did at least give protection to those in charge.

72. SS SIR RICHARD GRENVILLE

This unusual vessel was one of the Great Western Railway Company's passenger tender steamers, specially built to handle embarking and disembarking liner passengers and their luggage out in the Sound. She has plenty of saloon space below and a 'ferry-like' promenade deck above. Upon sale in 1964, this ship ran for a while for the Jersey Shipping Company, under the name *La Duchesse de Normandie*. During her years at Plymouth a running mate, the *Sir John Hawkins*, also tended the liners.

73. SS MENDIP

One of a series of ten similar steam colliers, *Mendip* 1,362g/1950 came into service under the control of the newly established British Electricity Authority resulting from the 1948 industry nationalisation. The ships were designed to bring power station coal south from Goole in Yorkshire to Poole, Prince Rock, Plymouth and Portishead installations. Their reign did not last long, as oil firing at some power stations made them redundant long before their time. Most had gone by 1960 but *Mendip* was retained until 1966 when, not only was she sold to the Italians but converted to a tanker with motor propulsion. She traded on for some years under the name of *Castelrosso*.

74. MV HIBERNIAN COAST

Coast Lines 'liner' service around the UK continued after WWII in much diminished form. Eventually, only two vessels remained on the London-Southampton-Plymouth-Liverpool service, and they had accommodation for just twelve passengers each. *Hibernian Coast* 1,258g/1947 and her sister ship succumbed to the roll-on, roll-off system of freight movement in the 1960s, and the passengers had forsaken them already. The Company's remaining cargo ship fleet was 'blended' with that of the once great General Steam Navigation Company, thus becoming part of the P & O Group of Companies.

Local Map No. 5   Plymouth to Saltash

(1) Cattedown Wharves
(2) Sutton Harbour
(3) Millbay Docks
(4) Stonehouse Pool
(5) Tamar Bridges

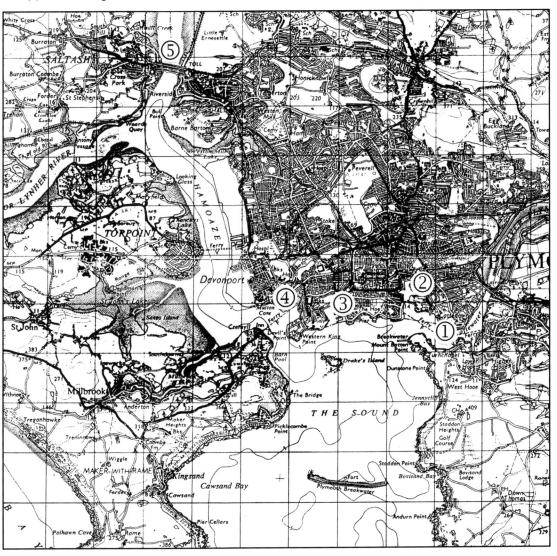

75. SS HEREFORD

WWII 'standard' cargo ships were still very much in evidence on the ocean trade routes in 1958. This particular example seen in Plymouth's Millbay Dock appears to be straight out of drydock, and as good as the day she was launched at Montreal in 1943. Devoid of topmasts yet still carrying her spindly WWII signal mast, and a heavy lift derrick, she shows the tiny wheelhouse windows of wartime tonnage – some protection for the navigation department in the event of being fired upon. *Hereford* 7,130 grt., started out as *Fort Ticonderoga* and rather unusually for 1958 had joined the Peoples Republic of China flag. With a deadweight tonnage of 10,384 no doubt she spent several more years tramping sedately at about 10kts. Three Scotch- type boilers, oil fired from 1950 onwards, fed steam to the triple expansion engine.

76. MT NAVIGO

The Swedish tanker *Navigo* 10,543g/16,755d/1992 is a good example of tanker tonnage built in the last couple of decades. Suitable for either chemicals or clean petroleum products, she has just discharged her cargo at Cattedown, and is now passing Sutton Harbour en route to the sea. For hose handling, modern tankers are fitted with hydraulic deck cranes in lieu of the old style derricks, and other recent changes include a gravity launched enclosed lifeboat at the stern, satellite communications, and a full width wheelhouse. All these items are now generally standard. Fort Batten provided this photograph viewpoint in 2007.

77. Off Sutton Harbour

One of Plymouth's local ferry / excursion boats is about to berth at Lambhay. On the left is the entrance to Sutton Harbour's fishing vessel base and yacht marina. The large white / glass building is the National Marine Aquarium.

78. The Eddystone Lighthouse

These dangerous offshore rocks received their first 'tentative' light tower in 1698 when Winstanley constructed his curiously designed wooden version. Designs soon became more successful, and better able to withstand the ferocious elements, and the present tower dates from 1882. It stands some 133ft high and exhibits two white flashes every 10 secs, visible for 17 miles. It is the fifth tower on this site, the previous version, Smeaton's of 1759, has been reconstructed on Plymouth Hoe. The image shows the stump of the previous tower and boat access in fair weather to the 1882 lighthouse.

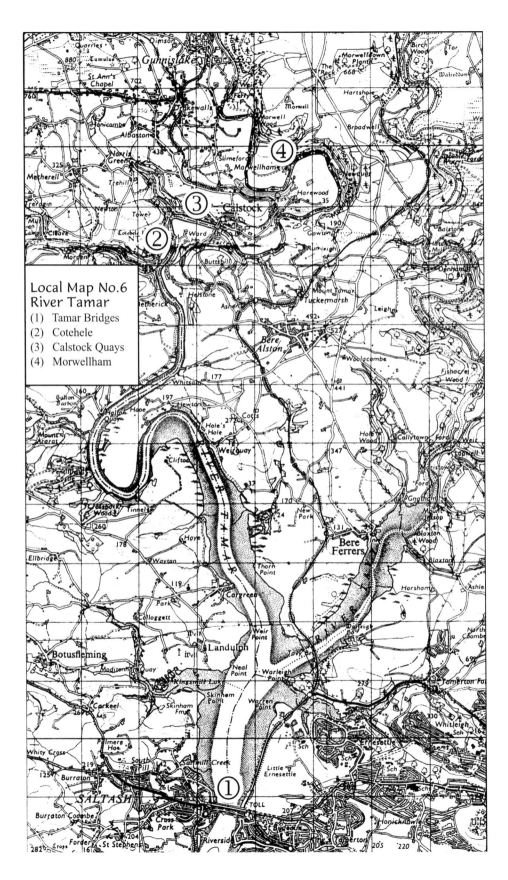

Local Map No.6
River Tamar

(1) Tamar Bridges
(2) Cotehele
(3) Calstock Quays
(4) Morwellham

79. GARLANDSTONE
at Morwellham Quay

Benedictine Monks founded this remote quay on the Devon side of the River Tamar over one thousand years ago. Its suitability for moving goods was plainly evident as roads and trackways in the area were nigh on non-existent. Woollen goods could now be sent down the twenty miles or so to Plymouth, and beyond. However it would be the full exploitation of mineral wealth discovered in the Tamar Valley that would lead to Morwellham's subsequent importance. Silver and lead ore were certainly extracted by 1300, and copper by the 1500s. Imported raw materials included timber, coal, sand and iron. At its peak in the mid to late 1800s some 700,000 tons of copper ore were produced along with 72,000 tons of the bi-product, arsenic. The ore extracted was largely shipped to South Wales for refining, by ketches and schooners, whilst other cargoes were locally handled by the Tamar sailing barges. Given suitable tides on the river, Morwellham Quays could accept ships up to about 300 tons capacity. In the 1860s some three hundred people lived and worked on site, and it was not unusual for up to 4,000 tons of ore to be piled on the quayside awaiting shipment. Discovery overseas of better grade ore deposits, the coming of the railways and the near exhaustion of local mine production, saw a dramatic decline in activity. In 1901, the complex was said to be deserted. Following years of abandonment to nature, in 1969 the Morwellham and Tamar Trust began restoring the dock, buildings, a mine and infrastructure to open to the public – a mammoth undertaking on the neglected site. Today, the trading ketch *Garlandstone* 54r/1909 built by James Goss at nearby Calstock, lies beautifully preserved in Morwellham's loading dock. She spent her trading years in the West Country and Irish Sea areas. The 2006 photograph shows some of the sections of overhead wagon ways from the mines.

80. SS ALBION at Calstock

Communication and movement of goods were made easy by the Tamar, and Calstock developed as an important 'inland' seaport. Although just a few miles down river from the subject of No.79, Calstock grew up on the Cornish bank of the river. The quays handled the products of mining, quarrying, brick making and agriculture, plus the river paddle steamer service of the Devon and Cornwall Steam Packet Company, who ran to Devonport. The railway arrived by way of a magnificent high concrete block viaduct in 1907, which is still in use today. Adjacent to the Calstock end of the viaduct a steam powered wagon hoist served to lower standard gauge wagons carrying stone, down to the quaysides for ship loading. Coastal steamers then shipped granite blocks away for such projects as Dover Harbour improvement. On the opposite bank (Devon side), James Goss' Shipyard built trading vessels including the already described *Garlandstone*.

The photograph dates from around 1905, and the steam coaster *Albion* 347g/1900 is loading granite blocks whilst beyond, schooners, brigantines and ketches await their turn to load. The regular paddle steamer hurries by and a Tamar sailing barge hand does a little 'poling' to help turn his craft. Note the wharf steam crane appears to share one rail with the wagon track.

81. Calstock Viaduct

The scene is in 2006 and Calstock's days of great industry are long gone. Ships no longer load at the quays and small recreational vessels now ply the Tamar. The lofty viaduct has just reached its century, and its once busy wagon hoist had been situated against the far side of the second archway from the right. Although the direction here is north-west, we are actually looking downstream towards the sea at this point, given those giant Tamar meanders.

82. SHAMROCK at Cotehele

Now a delightfully tranquil spot maintained by the National Trust, this quay served the needs of Cotehele House and Estate nearby. The lime kilns have been restored and in one building there is a good display of local shipping history. In the 2006 photograph, the Tamar barge *Shamrock* 32r/1899 is in finely restored condition and sits in the tiny incut river dock. Built at Stonehouse, Plymouth, she was known as an 'inside-the-breakwater' trader. In 1919 some modifications were undertaken to permit short coastal voyages and she was duly fitted with a 30hp paraffin motor, capable of pushing the little ketch along at 6 kts. Full restoration was carried out in 1981. Her last trading days were spent carrying roadstone from the Lizard to Falmouth.

General Map No. 3 Looe to Lands End to Bude

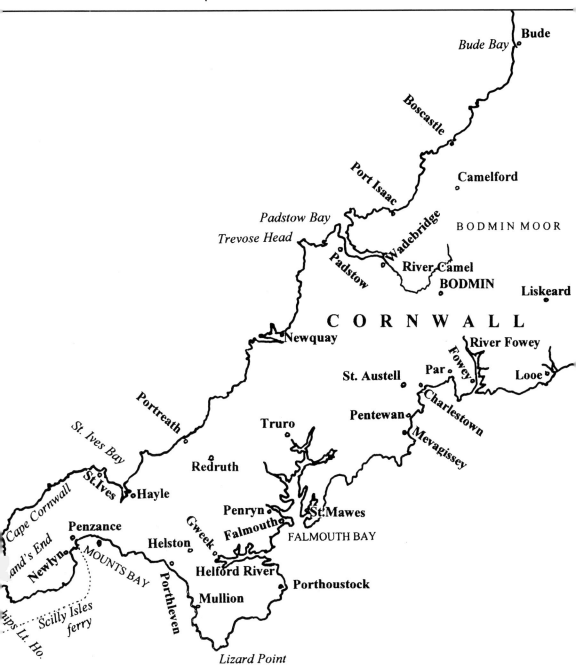

83. Looe Harbour entrance

Just entering harbour is a small topsail schooner with a local fishing boat astern, still under sail. The 1930s image shows men aloft taking in the schooners' sails, and she appears to be coming in to load. Looe has been a port since ancient times at the confluence of the East and West Looe Rivers. Granite, tin and copper ore were exported from the Caradon Mines complex north of Liskeard. In 1828 a canal enabled small barges to bring ores down to Looe from Moorswater, near Liskeard, but the advent of the railway alongside the canal saw this unnecessary trans-shipment stage eliminated in 1860. By 1917 the Caradon Mines were closed. As with many minor West Country harbours sailing ships were built and owned here, but the shallow nature and width of the harbour would only permit access to vessels up to about 150ft in length, and some 10ft draught on spring tides, ie, 300 to 400 ton ships. Today Looe thrives as an inshore 'day-boat' fishing base - out on one tide, and back on the next, with very fresh fish to land at the local market. Tourism is now also highly important to this Cornish town's prosperity.

← 84. Looe, inner harbour

At low water this 2007 view clearly shows the nature of the place. Small craft abound and together with a couple of the inshore fishing vessels over against the Fish Market, all await the twice daily incoming tide to get underway. The railway still runs down from Liskeard to Looe Station, on the right hand bank beyond the old stone bridge. In earlier years, coal for local consumption and especially mining machinery would have been a major import.

85. ST GALLANT

Moving on to Fowey, we see the crew of the smart little tug *Gallant* 69g/1884 posing for the camera. She was built at Rye, East Sussex where no great iron ship building had previously been attempted, or indeed, much afterwards. However, this little vessel was a great success. Bate of Fowey first owned her, and she would then remain in the port for seventy years! Finally, Fowey Harbour Commissioners sold her in 1954 to Reynolds of Tor Point, and she remained in service at Plymouth until scrapping in 1964. Back in 1903 *Gallant* had been lengthened by 9ft and her tonnage increased to 76. Fowey and neighbouring ports involvement in the massive china clay industry is next examined.

China Clay

Cornwall's enormous mineral wealth had been exploited for a thousand years before William Cookworthy, a Devon man discovered china clay deposits in 1746. No longer would China have the sole ability to produce fine porcelain. Within a few decades the now familiar 'lunar landscape' of giant pits and mountains of spoil around St.Austell began to materialise. China clay (or Kaolin) evolved naturally over the millennia as water action gradually 'rotted' granite down to finer particles. Extraction by way of high pressure water jets enabled the removal of sand and stones, thereby leaving the basic clay. This could then be repeatedly washed and settled out before going to the 'dries'. The final dry, white product would then be shipped as required. At first, small trading ships beached wherever possible to load ashore in the time honoured way – all dependent on weather, suitable tides and water depth. Proper wharves and quays soon appeared in sheltered harbours to handle ever increasing tonnages of the much sought after material, and the next three locations visited have all played a major role, with that of Fowey continuing to this day. In recent decades a quantity of china clay has been exported in 'slurry' form in specialist ships. From 1861 rail movement of clay in bulk to the ports arrived when the Great Western Railway percolated to the area, and duly controlled eight china clay loading berths at Fowey. By the 1930s three of the berths were fitted with direct conveyor loading facilities for the ships, and steamers up to around 10,000 tons could be accommodated. Other berths had crane or spout loading for the ships. In 1962 nearly 500,000 tons of clay departed overseas and in 1983 some 1,154,522 tons left in ships up to 12,000 tons capacity. China clay became ever more useful in modern times in a number of manufacturing processes. Its purity enabled inclusion as a base material in paper making, textiles, chemicals, cosmetics, shaving soap, paint and even medicines.

Turning to Fowey, the deep water well sheltered anchorage had been recognised long before 1200. From the 1600s to as late as 1930, the Newfoundland salt cod trade had been a major employer for locally owned ships. General goods went out to the Mediterranean, thence salt to Newfoundland, with the salted cod on the return leg – a very profitable triangular pattern of trade with no voyage leg in ballast. John Stephens ran a fleet of schooners locally, in this traffic. This harbour also witnessed merchantmen in lay-up during the depression years of the twenties and thirties, and up to a dozen such ships would on occasion be awaiting better times. Today, apart from continuing to handle some china clay, the port sees the occasional cruise ship visit and yachting is ever popular.

86. SS HARMODIUS

In this 1920s scene *Harmodius* 5,229g/1919 is riding high and the dust surrounding No.1 hold shows that china clay loading had not long started at Fowey's No.4 jetty. This steamer belonged to the British & South American Steam Navigation Company of Liverpool. Built at Irvine, Scotland she could carry about 8,000 tons of just about most things on offer in the tramping trades, and it is likely that coal out and grain home were regular contenders. The holds would need to be clean and dry for this loading. Over to the right and moored with her own bow anchors is a large sailing vessel, one of a rapidly diminishing number at this period.

87. SS ANTONIO DE SATRUSTEGUI

Waiting to load clay is a ship with a very long name and equally long career. This veteran Spanish steamer began life in Canada under the name *Canadian Raider* 3,289g/1920, and she survived until the late 1970s – a tribute to her builders and careful owners. From 1957 oil firing replaced coal for the boilers and latterly she was radar fitted. In the photograph at Fowey, the holds have been cleaned, dried and readied for the 'white stuff' and any anticipated shower will be kept out by lifted tarpaulins over the hatchways. Between 1965 and the end of 1976 the old ship carried some 200,000 tons of china clay to Italy during 48 voyages. One of the last of her type still trading, three scotch boilers supplied steam for her triple expansion engine.

88. MTs DUNHERON & GRIBBEN HEAD

The Fowey Harbour Commissioners operate tugs to assist the berthing operations at the china clay jetties. In this fine photograph the *Gribben Head* 132g/1955 is moving on to pastures new in tow of the near identical *Dunheron*. In this 1988 scene the pair are passing the castle remains at Polruan, on their way out to sea. *Gribben Head* put in twenty years service at Fowey.

89. MV NORDANHAV

A far cry from the grace of the sailing ships or even the appeal of the steamers, the box-like hull of this ship is devoid of sheer altogether. Travelling, tracked gantries remove hatch cover slabs to the vast holds, and an amidships form of self-discharging gear with a long unloading arm is fitted. Everything about this ship indicates functionality in today's fierce economic climate. *Nordanhav* 5,993g/1992 is Swedish owned and Dutch flagged and would lift a cargo of just under 10,000 tons.

90. Fowey-Bodinnick Ferry

The ferry is seen here in Spring 2007 heading across the Fowey River to the Bodinnick side with some of the china clay jetties visible upstream. Records state that a 'Charter Ferry' was running here in the year 1100. In the 1950s two small 'floating bridge' type ferries, one for 6 cars, the other for just 2, were in action, powered by 15hp motor launches. Today, the modern equivalent is much more substantial and of some importance in avoiding a long road detour. An ambulance will be first down the ramp. Beyond, loading clay, is the coaster *Jorvik* 2,450g/2000.

91.   MV SHEILA HAMMANN at Par →

Beach loading of ships with granite and copper ore had taken place here long before the first tentative steps were made towards construction of a proper harbour, in 1829. Par became connected to Fowey by the Cornish Minerals Railway, and the original hope had been for iron ore exporting. This traffic failed to materialise but china clay soon filled the gap. Par would become a ship building, repairing and owning port and in 1885, 86,000 tons of china clay departed. By 1962 it was nearer 750,000 tons when some 1,500 vessels visited. The port's depth would only permit vessels up to around 1,200 tons deadweight to load and therefore it served the coastal and European sector. In the 1950s and 1960s large numbers of Dutch and German coasters would bring Baltic timber to South Coast ports and then make the short ballast trip to Par to load china clay for the voyage back to Northern Europe. In this photograph the German L.A.D. type coaster, *Sheila Hammann* 1,022g/1983 awaits her turn to load. During 2007 it was reported that operations at Par were drawing to a close, for as already mentioned, other overseas sources of china clay are having an effect on Cornwall's once mighty industry.

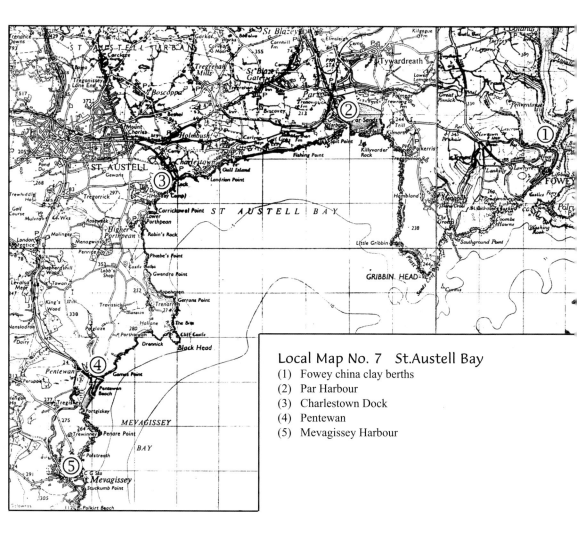

Local Map No. 7   St.Austell Bay
(1)   Fowey china clay berths
(2)   Par Harbour
(3)   Charlestown Dock
(4)   Pentewan
(5)   Mevagissey Harbour

92. SS SIR JAMES at Charlestown

The third of the local china clay ports recently active is Charlestown which was completed in 1801 to export copper ore – it soon went over to china clay handling. The original dock remains completely intact today, with vessels always remaining afloat by way of a single set of gates. The outer harbour is strictly tidal and dries out well beyond the dock entrance at low water. Vessels entered bow first to load or unload, and had to be warped back out astern, on their own ropes, to make their departure. The dock was too narrow for ships to be turned round in port. Originally, a number of local industries were served, including a small shipyard, brickworks, limekilns and a fishery. As late as 1983 apart from china clay exports, other cargoes included general, grain, and coal which had previously featured prominently. Charlestown's clay export figures seemed remarkably constant over a very long period – about 60,000 tons per annum – all shipped out in small vessels of just a few hundred tons capacity. The last clay cargo sailed just a few years ago and the port has become something of a tourist attraction and the base for Square Sail's fleet of sailing vessels much used in the 'period' film industry. In this 1950s scene, the tiny ex victualling steam lighter, *Sir James* 146g/1945 is moored not far from one of the clay chutes, visible beyond her mast.

93. MV FREMA

A photograph from the 1950s and a typical Dutch '200' tonner is warping through the outer harbour, in laden condition. *Frema* 197g/1931 could lift about 270 tons of cargo and just visible out in the bay, another similar craft awaits her turn to enter port.

94. MVs INSISTENCE & TARQUENCE

Two of the London and Rochester Company's (Crescent Shipping) motor coasters are seen here loading china clay from Charlestown's chute system. A good pile of the white stuff can be seen ever growing in the *Insistence's* single box-like hold, as she nears her loadline marks. This ship, 475g/1975 and her slightly newer sister vessel were lengthened after a few years to help extend their competitive lives, and this operation gave a tonnage of 644 gross. The procedure was carried out on a number of the fleet units.

95. Charlestown Dock in 2007

Apart from a few cars and modern boats visible, the effect obtained hereabouts is almost an 'ageless' one. Square Sail's vessels and attendant quayside paraphernalia of wooden barrels, crates and old fashioned lobster pots, all go towards creating that period look. The fact that a constant stream of small merchant ships entered to load china clay, and departed stern first, now seems all the more amazing. One of the old loading chutes has been retained as part of the fine Heritage Centre established beyond, dedicated to the history of Charlestown and local china clay handling

96. IMOGENE at Pentewan

A little further down the coast from Charlestown there existed another port similarly intended for exporting minerals. Pentewan was completed in 1826 and also soon became involved in the clay trade. This harbour, sadly, is one that genuinely was built in the wrong place. It suffered from the outset with serious siltation problems and by the end of WWI the china clay trade had gone. After a final burst of activity between the wars when concrete blocks were manufactured and despatched by sea, nature gained the upper hand, and closure inevitably happened in the 1940s. The port's infrastructure is today remarkably intact, as if frozen in time by the ever encroaching sand. However, in this fine image from 1914 the barquentine *Imogene* 177r/1891, built at Troon and owned in Fowey, sits in the dock along with other local craft. The elevated wagonway with loading chutes raised can be clearly seen alongside the quay. In Nos 97/98 we shall see the reason for closure.

97. Pentewan Basin in 2007

The dock basin remains full of water today, and the gates are still in situ as if the last ship has just left. This harbour basin and entrance were actually constructed to larger dimensions than the nearby successful Charlestown dock. Just visible bottom right, is a wall built close to the gates to prevent further problems arising. The build up of sand is quite phenomenal. The ships seen in No.96, the 1914 photograph were moored along the left hand quay, just inside the gates.

98. 'Sand choked' in 2007

The sandy area was once the channel from the sea up to the dock gates, just visible left centre. The basin lies behind the hill on the right. Several hundred yards of sand now preclude any form of craft from visiting Pentewan, and the feint line in the sand is simply matting put down for folk to walk upon to the sea, some considerable distance behind the camera.

99. LADY ST. JOHNS at Mevagissey

This fine harbour dates back many centuries and was not conceived as a 'mineral' port, but simply as a fishing community. In the 1400s the first pier was built, but those enclosing the present inner harbour date from 1775. Outer piers giving better protection were completed in 1897. An in depth study of local fishing boats is not really within the remit of this work, but briefly, Mevagissey's substantial fleet consisted of 40ft sailing luggers and smaller half-length 'toshers' for long lining. Some general trade in schooners and ketches saw coal brought inwards, along with barrels to fill with pilchards, for export. Ships up to about 200 tons could visit the port and in the photograph, the Kingsbridge built topsail schooner *Lady St.Johns* 114r/1898 is probably unloading coal, on what appears to be a wet day. A large old canvas has been vertically rigged above the ship's hatchway, and a 'wishbone' gaff with gin readied for unloading cargo, in its shelter. Note the Fowey registered lugger in the foreground.

100. Mevagissey in 2007

The scene across a sunny inner harbour shows inshore fishing boats and a smattering of leisure craft. Both these categories, together with the delightful charm of the place for visiting tourists, now ensure prosperity.

101. INDUSTRY at Truro

Our trip resumes in the City of Truro before journeying down to Falmouth. The Rivers Kenwyn and Allen join at Truro, becoming known as the Truro River until joining the Tresillian and the Fal, thus broadening out into Carrick Roads above Falmouth. Small trading ships have reached quays at Truro for hundreds of years and certainly served tin works in the fourteenth century. Coast Lines built a large warehouse to serve their network of routes and, in the 1930s, coal, grain, slag, timber and building materials were imported, and some clay exported. Ships up to about 1,000 tons capacity could be accommodated but by 1982 a mere five ships visited, handling just 4,630 tons of cargo. Today, a quay at Newham, opposite Boscawen Park a short distance down river from Truro City, handles some bulk cargoes when tides allow. In the 1916 image, the local sailing ketch barge *Industry* 27r/1889 is awaiting a rise of tide. This whole area has in recent years been totally redeveloped, and is now largely covered by parking facilities, shops and pedestrian walkways.

102. (ex.) PS COMPTON CASTLE

The view in No.101 would have been taken somewhere to the left of this photograph, and a tiny bit of the concrete river retaining wall is still visible. With the customary high street names appearing beyond, this part of the River Allen has been largely covered over, and is now a permanent home to the old River Dart paddle steamer *Compton Castle* 97g/1914. She is currently serving as a florist shop and was originally an earlier sister vessel to the *Kingswear Castle* described in No.51.

103. Truro's Old Port

This view is the reverse from the bridge astern of the *Compton Castle* in No.102. Just a few decades ago warehouses on the banks here were handling cargoes to and from Dutch and British motor coasters. Now, designer offices and apartments prevail whilst on high, Truro School tower still presides, peering through the trees. Coast Lines warehouse was right on the confluence of the Allen and Kenwyn Rivers, just to the left of the two masted boat in this 2007 scene.

104. MB DICTION

Seen in lay-up along the riverbank just south of Truro in Spring 2007 and a long way from her original trading haunts, is the ex- London and Rochester Company motor barge *Diction* 189g/1963. She and many similar sized sister ships, had to all intents and purposes been the logical successors to the Thames and Medway sailing barges. This example came to Cornwall to operate in the specialist calcified seaweed dredging trade, from Truro.

105. MV SUSANNA

Loading scrap metal by hydraulic crane at Truro in 2007 is the German operated L.A.D. motor coaster *Susanna* 1,512g/1980. She trades for Erwin Strahlman under the 'ECHOSHIP' banner and is a member of a growing fleet of such vessels trading around Europe. Individual slab hatch covers can be seen stacked at each end of the long, high coaming, style hatchway. The emblem beneath the ship's name indicates the presence of a bow thruster, for good manoeuvrability in port. The ship is berthed just below a sluice gate arrangement designed to help maintain water depth below this point for shipping. The upper reaches at Truro are now somewhat silted.

106. KING HARRY FERRY in the 1920s

A peaceful scene across the river as the old ferry raises steam in anticipation of the next crossing. A rudimentary shelter exists on deck, mercifully not too adjacent to the boiler room, and no doubt farm animals, carts and the like were more frequent than private cars. A deeply laden local sailing barge is moored nearby with a couple of boats alongside, and the occasional passing vessel en route to Truro, would make an interesting distraction.

← 107.   KING HARRY FERRY in 2007

The incumbent motor ferry on the route today is certainly a major technological advance on that seen in No.106. Capable of transporting up to around 32 cars, it now makes frequent crossings, especially in Summer when the tourist traffic likes to avoid the long detour to reach the Roseland Peninsula, from the Falmouth side. With the Cornish flag flying above the 'bridge' – wheelhouse would be somewhat inappropriate on a chain ferry – the next vehicle queue is forming on the far side.

Falmouth

This expansive safe haven had been used for centuries long before Falmouth developed as a town. Around 1600 the established ports of Truro, Penryn and Helston were apparently outraged at Falmouth's sudden rise in importance, two in particular previously had municipal jurisdiction over the new 'upstart'. Quay construction began in the late 1700s and the first Post Office packet service started to Lisbon. By 1827 packet boats were running to North and South America. Steam power would see the eventual loss of the Post Office contracts to Plymouth and Southampton.

Falmouth's strategic position at the western end of the English Channel has always encouraged 'refuge' access for all classes of vessel in need of repair, and in the pre-wireless era, homecoming merchantmen would put in to receive their owner's discharge port orders. These services required the liaison work of the port's many shipping agents. The basic shape of today's drydock and repair facilities evolved around 1860. It is for the ship repairing, voyage maintenance and dry docking work that the port is best known. There were also a number of local ship builders of wooden, iron and steel vessels. Cargo traffic has never been particularly heavy, although coal for the gas works, industrial and domestic use and later, oil and some bulk commodities have been handled.

Another activity of some significance has been the lay-up of merchant ships, either due to recession in trade, or simply changing hands during their careers. The Fal's sheltered deep water valleys are ideal for this function. Merchant ships of many types have changed hands at Falmouth to re-join trade with new owners, and of course the ability to perform 'docking sales' for underwater hull surveys and painting, make the location most attractive. In the height of the 1920s-1930s depression some 35 ships were in lay-up in the Truro River, and another 20 or so, lower down on the Fal. Mention must be made of Penryn, once by far the senior port to Falmouth. At the head of the short, navigable Penryn River, quays had prospered here for centuries. In 1652 the Custom House moved round to Falmouth in recognition of that town's growing prosperity. Recent decades have seen coal and agricultural cargoes handled at Penryn, with some granite exported. The harbour dries at low water and today depends largely on the yachting industry.

← 108.   Prince of Wales Pier, Falmouth

Local ferry and excursion steamers abound at the pier in this view from the early 1900s, whilst beyond a variety of steam tugs and small wooden craft sit peacefully on their moorings. The white hulled steamer *Victoria* 68g/1901 is nearest and ran for the River Fal S.S.Co. Angled to the berth just astern of her is the little *Roseland* 41g/1886, locally built, and run by the St.Mawes Steam Tug and Passenger Co. The third vessel this side of the pier is the Falmouth built *Victor* 153g/1898. Finally, just visible by the funnel top is *Alexandra* 73g/1902, also locally built.

← 109. Prince of Wales Pier in 2007

About a century later and excursion vessels and ferries still make the pier a busy place. *Enterprise*, the nearest boat is due to sail at 14.30 for Truro and Malpas. *Pride of Falmouth* lies just astern, and another small excursion boat is moored a short way off the pier.

← 110. Falmouth Docks

This is a 1930s view across to the docks and a number of ocean going vessels are in for repair and attention. Two ocean tankers are visible far left and the one on the pier near the dredger is a unit of the British Tanker Co. fleet. In 1933 some 54 tankers in the 6,000-12,000 ton range were trading for the forerunners of B.P. Two Federal Steam Navigation Company ships can also be made out by their funnels, and they were much involved in the refrigerated meat trade from Australia and New Zealand to the UK via the Panama Canal. The firm was consolidated in 1895, and taken over by the New Zealand Shipping Company in 1912, part of the P & O Group.

111. CUTTY SARK

This famous old composite built clipper, 963g/1869 was built at Dumbarton for Captain John Willis, a London ship owner, and was soon regarded as one of the fastest in the China tea trade. By the early 1880s she had switched to the Australian wool trade, and still made some remarkably quick passages. In 1895 she left British registry to trade under the Portuguese flag as *Ferreira,* and before 1922 carried the name *Maria de Ampero*. That year saw the ship return to Britain when purchased and re-rigged by Captain Wilfred H. Dowman, to serve as a stationary training ship at Falmouth. She made a brief voyage under tow in August 1924 to Fowey to act as the local regatta flagship. Her final sea passage was under tow in 1938 when she went to the Thames at Greenhithe to be similarly employed by the Thames Nautical Training School. The end of 1954 saw the ultimate move to the special drydock at Greenwich where she has been on Public display ever since.

Of course, it has now become necessary to add a sad postscript to the saga, as early in 2007, whilst undergoing major restoration work, a serious fire swept through the ship. Fortunately a major portion of the ship's gear, artefacts and some structure had already been removed for conservation, so it is to be hoped that she can rise once more to grace the Greenwich skyline. Such an important piece of Britain's maritime heritage must be saved. The photograph from around 1924 shows *Cutty Sark* moored in her training ship role at Falmouth.

112. REGINA at Custom House Quay

One 1930s motor car is visible here as the crew of the
local ketch *Regina* 39r/1897 ease the vessel out of the
little dock. A typical West Country local trader, she
was running at the time for Steed Bros.Ltd., Notter
Quay Quarries, St.Germans. Auxiliary motor power
had already been fitted in the form of a 30hp engine.
Falmouth's local gasworks gasometers can be seen,
left distant.

113. Customs House Quay in 2007 →

The view in No.112 but some seventy years later,
and the enormous increase in leisure boating is
much apparent. Diverse modern craft now lay about
at their moorings, and spotting any with traditional
wooden hulls is becoming increasingly difficult
as the years pass. Motor vehicles are less of an
observational problem!

114. SS KENT & ST. MAWES →

Federal Tankers' *Kent* 31,763d/1960 is seen here arriving under tow from the Isle of Grain in 1968, following
earlier major engine room woes. One of the Falmouth Towage Company's steam tugs, *St.Mawes* 346g/1951
is already positioned off the starboard bow as the ship passes St.Anthonys Head lighthouse, en route to the
Drydocks. *Kent* left the P & O Group at this time to trade for overseas owners, under the name of *Lesley Ann
Conway.*

115.   STs ST. DENYS & ST. AGNES

Assisting in berthing *Kent* alongside the tank cleaning jetty at Falmouth, shortly after No.114 was taken, are two more units of Falmouth Towage's steam tug fleet, the *St. Denys* 174g/1929 and *St. Agnes* 226g/1925. The entrances to the various drydocks can be seen beyond the tugs.

116.   SS QUILOA in drydock →

It is 1969, and Trident Tankers' *Quiloa* 13,113g/1960, a clean oil products tanker is in drydock. She was one of a pair originally built for the British India Steam Navigation Company at a time when individual P & O Companies started diversifying into the tanker trades. The ship was in drydock for underwater attention plus the replacement of her high pressure steam turbine rotor, which had earlier failed. *Quiloa* and sister ship *Queda,* ran under charter to BP for many years in the Worldwide clean oil trades. In this view forward from the midships bridge, on the foredeck just beyond the foremast can be seen the large hinged hatch cover to the ship's dry cargo hold. Some tankers at this time still carried drum cargo to remote outlying ports where little or no bulk storage facilities existed. This was a throwback to the days when case oil was carried in conventional cargo ships before the advent of dedicated oil tankers.

117.   SS QUILOA (aft view) →

This image, taken straight after No.116, shows the after end of the ship with Carrick Roads beyond. The cargo tank hatch lids are wide open as the tanks have been gas freed and certified as such, by the Port Chemist for the docking and repair work. This ship was standard in layout with the deck officers accommodated amidships, and the engineering officers and crew, aft. One area in which these ships were already rather out dated was in the provision of two separate cargo pumprooms, one forward and one on the maindeck, each fitted with steam reciprocating pumps. These drew cargo from the 27 cargo tanks by way of a double ring-main pipeline system, and double shut-off valves were fitted everywhere to segregate oil grades carried. Subsequently, the majority of tankers were built with a single after pumproom, whereby steam turbines in the engine room could power the centrifugal type pumps in the pumproom, adjacent. Steam cranes still ran on the Drydock railway system at this time, and your Author had reached the dizzy rank of 3rd.Officer.

← 118. MV GOLDEN DOLPHIN

Seen in lay-up in the River Fal around 1983 is the Greek owned refrigerated cargo ship *Golden Dolphin* 16,275g/1968. She started trading as Port Lines' *Port Caroline* on the Australia-New Zealand-UK route, and at the time of her construction would have been considered a very large ship of her type. From the 1970s onwards, many traditional cargo ships would not see out their potential lifespan with British owners, as the rush to containerise trades was underway. Many top quality ships were simply laid up, sold overseas or even sent to the breakers. This ship shows the transition from conventional derricks to deck cranes for cargo handling, as she was fitted with a liberal selection of both.

← 119. MV CRESTBANK

The former Bank Line cargo liner *Crestbank* 12,234g/1978 was another ship made redundant before her time, and had been a member of a very large fleet of similar vessels. The peak of midships bridge ship design, had been reached at the time of her construction and traditional, robust cargo derricks fitted. She lasted but eight years under her first name then had four more, but was not scrapped until 2006. The photograph dates from 1986.

120. MV PRIDE OF KENT

A similar background scene to No.117, but this 2007 view shows P & O's Dover-Calais roll-on, roll-off ferry *Pride of Kent* 30,635g/1992, in for her annual docking. This ship began trading as the freight ferry *European Highway* of 22,986 grt. Later rebuilt with full passenger accommodation, her gross tonnage rose significantly as a result. The two level bow access arrangement can be clearly seen in this photograph. Over to the right the French flag tanker *Adour* 8,550g/2003 is berthed. *Pride of Kent's* full width bridge and large windows make a fascinating comparison to such provided to early powered vessels. Ship owners, always a conservative bunch, considered it necessary for their Masters and Navigating Officers to be totally out in the open – as in sailing ship days – in order to execute their duties correctly. Today, of course wheelhouses are literally stuffed with electronic equipment, which performs best in constant temperature and air conditioned splendour. Thanks to radar and satellite navigation systems, knowing where one is and what's around and about, is generally no longer in doubt. However, the requirement for a vigilant look-out will never diminish.

← 121. Porthoustock, old stone chutes

Stone has been quarried for centuries in this remote part of the Lizard. Porthoustock was just a tiny fishing hamlet and cove when, many decades ago, a stone loading facility was constructed. The photograph shows a long since abandoned jetty structure with eight chute remains still visible. These would have been suitable for loading the smallest coastal craft of the day. A much larger concrete structure was later erected on the opposite side of the cove to load coasters, but this closed in 1958, and was later demolished. Today, stone loading has resumed here after wharf improvements. See No.122.

← 122. MV SAMAKI

Photographed against the early morning sun in April 2007 is the little motor coaster *Samaki* 494g/1966, loading roadstone at Porthoustock by way of an elevator system kept topped up by hydraulic bucket crane from the stockpile. Loading ships in such isolated, exposed locations is naturally weather and tide dependent, but has to be the only sensible option where roads are restricted. Coasters of this size are rare today, and it is also encouraging to see that road haulage does not have everything its own way.

123. Dean Quarry

This is the view over Dean Quarry from the South West coastal path, just west of Porthoustock. Despite offshore reefs, rocks and wrecks ships managed to call in to the little jetty for decades to load stone. At one time an extension to the jetty was reportedly made by sinking the hull of an old sailing barge, although a proper piling job was later carried out. Vessels coming here to load first had to pick up a Pilot off Falmouth, before attempting to berth on the incoming tide. Loading was rapid over high water, and departure vital before the tide dropped, to avoid hull damage. This procedure similarly prevails at Porthoustock.

124. The Lizard Lighthouse

The long Lizard peninsula jutting miles out into the English Channel has always been a major hazard for shipping, and especially during the sailing ship era when poor weather claimed many. The first lighthouse was established in 1619 and the present operational tower dates from 1752. At a height of some 230ft above sea level, the white light flashes every 3 secs, and is visible for 25 miles.

125. Penzance Harbour →

First recognised as a fishing port in Tudor times, Penzance became a major tin exporter in the seventeenth century. The first proper pier dated from 1766 with subsequent improvements being made by 1812. Albert Pier was completed in 1853 and an inner floating harbour followed in 1880 with Holman's Drydock, which is still in use. In the 1930s coastal trade consisted of imports of coal, timber, grain, tallow and hemp, whilst exports were copper, tin, granite, some china clay, fish and potatoes. The long running Scilly Isles passenger and freight service is based here. Vessels of about 2,000 tons can enter the port. In this early 1900s distant view over the port, a number of ships are moored along the piers and one very elderly looking three masted sailing ship sits awkwardly in the middle of the harbour. Just discernible middle left is one larger steamship, possibly even the subject of No.126, The local gasworks gasometers also clearly show.

126. SS COATH →

The Penzance shipowner George Bazely started running ships in 1875 with just one schooner to link with his business interests in Swansea and Cardiff. By 1880 he ran a fleet of four ships in the cargo and passenger, London to Bristol service via Penzance and other West Country harbours. The Company also became known as The Little Western S.S. Co. and in 1897 the ex Clyde Shipping steamer *Skerryvore* 975g/1882 was acquired and renamed *Coath*. She traded until sold in 1915 and was later reported as missing during a WWI munitions run from Newhaven Harbour. Coast Lines took over Little Western's remaining ships and trade in 1920. The photograph probably dates from just before WWI, and shows the ship in the River Avon. Close examination of the ship reveals some fascinating detail. The navigating bridge is totally open and unprotected save for the inevitable freshly whitened canvas spray 'dodger'. Portholes and ventilator cowl rings are brass, and polished! The ship has very little in the way of deck houses, but a good number of portholes at maindeck level. Just discernible are a number of pairs of large doors along the hull side, between the forecastle and bridge areas – so the ship must have a very deep well deck forward, upon which the forward hatch is built. Possibly cattle stalls were used around this well deck when the vessel served in Scotland.

127. SS SCILLONIAN (1)

The essential connection between Penzance and Hughtown in the Scillies had been by sailing vessel until the 1850s when the first steamer went into service. In 1907 the present Isles of Scilly Steamship Company came into being, but it was not until 1926 that a specially built steamer arrived for the route, the first *Scillonian* 429grt, took over the mails and passenger traffic. In the photograph from around 1930, the Troon built steamer is in the customary berth at Penzance, awaiting the day's departure time.

128. MV SCILLONIAN (2)

The 1956 Southampton built version was this 921grt motor ship, a considerable advance on her predecessor. With improved derricks for handling Island supplies, the rugged hull design would be well suited to the often rough water crossing. This ship had her builder, Thorneycroft's distinctive louvred funnel top design. Propulsion was by Ruston & Hornsby oil engines driving twin screws. Passenger facilities included a bar and cafe to ease the two and a half hour crossing.

129. MV QUEEN OF THE ISLES

In 1965, an additional slightly smaller ship was ordered to run with *Scillonian* and she would be named *Queen of the Isles*, measuring in at 529 grt. A single hold served by one ten ton derrick differentiated her from the other vessel, and she could accommodate just 300 passengers. This ship's career on the Scillies run was not however to last, and by the 1970s she was deemed redundant, and subsequently gifted to the people of the Pacific Island of Tonga, by the Ministry of Overseas Development. She was reportedly derelict by 2001.

130. MV SCILLONIAN (3)

Seen loading at Penzance in spring 2007 is the third vessel of the name,1,256g/1977 representing a further size increase for the route. The two piece hinged hatch cover can be seen raised in front of the bridge, and a modern electric deck crane does the cargo work. This ship was constructed at Appledore, North Devon. Cargo traffic has increased over the years to the Scillies, and a specialist freight ferry/part tanker called *Gry Maritha* 590g/1981 now handles that side of the business, and acts as reserve ship.

131. Penzance inner harbour in 2007

The church tower gives a good reference point to compare with No.125. The view across the harbour shows the swingbridge allowing access to the inner basin beyond the road. The drydock runs parallel to the large sheds.

132. Newlyn South Pier →

Part of the original fifteenth century pier still exists within this much expanded fishing harbour. Major works were undertaken in the late nineteenth, and again in the twentieth century to further accommodate trawlers locally based, and visiting from elsewhere. In the 1930s photograph, a steam coaster is berthed at the South Pier quarry stone loading facility. This served as the outlet for stone quarried at nearby Penlee for many decades. Originally brought along the shore direct from the quarry by an industrial railway, ships of up to about 3,000 tons capacity could be loaded. A long line of rail hoppers can be seen on the pier. The facility closed around 1986. Newlyn is still an important fishing harbour.

133. MFV (PZ512) CORNISHMAN →

Taken in 2007, this scene aims to show the same location as No.132, some seventy years earlier. The pier has now long lost its visiting stone loading coasters, yet the wall, road, buildings and even the power cables have not altered that much. The Dutch built trawler PZ 512 *Cornishman,* is up on the slipway for underwater attention.

134. Newlyn Harbour in 2007

This general view of the modern harbour facilities for trawlers and inshore fishing vessels shows craft of all shapes and sizes. In the eighteenth and nineteenth centuries pilchard, mackerel and herring had been the main catch landed.

135. Lands End and Longships Lighthouse →

Having reached our westerly limit along the Channel coast, it seems appropriate to mark the turning point properly. In this delightful image, probably from the 1930s, a steam coaster is shaving a few miles off its voyage around Lands End. She is passing between the rugged rocks off Lands End, and the Longships Lighthouse. Deep sea sailormen often referred to the coastermen as 'rock-hoppers', and here one can see why! The tower dates from 1873 and at 115ft above sea level, an Iso. 10 secs light is exhibited – (equal 'on-off' period). The regulation three Trinity House light keepers were no doubt watching the passage of the coaster with interest, but it was obviously fine, calm weather. It would be many more decades before their important job would be replaced by remote automatic shore monitoring. Periodic brief flying visits by maintenance men in helicopters now ensure reliability, and the last old style keepers were phased out in the 1990s.

136. SS ISLESMAN →

Most definitely not qualifying as a "dirty British coaster with a salt-caked smoke stack", is the little steamer *Islesman* 281g/1904. She survived in the punishing coastal trades until the early 1950s when this image was taken. It would seem that the ship has just had a major overhaul and everything looks very 'shipshape'. A ladder for shore access is placed precisely on the centre of number two hatch. The masthead oil navigation lamp holder is freshly white painted, and ready to hoist on the guide wires. Some very tidy looking fendering has been placed over the starboard bow ready to push into some harbour tight spot. Only one item is missing, – the forward derrick. Although evidently now 'conned' from the chartroom below, the open bridge still sports that canvas spray dodger. No smoke from the boiler is showing as the old 47hp steam reciprocating engine does its stuff. Someone cared – a lot!

137. ELWOOD at St. Ives

The first pier constructed in the 1400s served to protect the fishing boats. As with many such early structures, storm damage regularly demanded repair. In 1770 the outer pier was completed to John Smeaton's design, and was followed in 1894 by the west pier, from which locally quarried stone would be shipped. Tin and copper were exported and general trade flourished. St Ives always was best known for its massive pilchard fishery, employing hundreds locally. Today the town is well known for artists and tourists, whilst fishing continues in much reduced form. The name of St.Ives was long seen on the sterns of a variety of ship types as a port of registry. Locally, from 1833 Edward Hain would develop his fleet of sailing ships. This long lived enterprise continued with steam ships, and then motor powered ocean traders, none of which could ever have visited their home port. His first powered craft was the *Trewidden* of 1873, and by 1917 when acquired by the P & O Group, the fleet totalled 27 steamers. Hain's suffered terribly from losses in both World wars, but the ships were soon replaced and continued under the Hain banner until merged into Hain-Nourse in the 1960s, and finally P & O General Cargo Division in the 1970s. In the photograph from1895, the topsail schooner *Elwood* 105r/1877, a product of Prince Edward Island, sits on the foreshore for attention with main topmast lowered. She was owned by John Hollow of St.Ives, and subsequently lost at the end of 1905.

138. Working craft at St. Ives ↗

The harbour is packed with sailing vessels in this image from the 1890s. Nearest the camera are three topsail trading schooners, whilst the majority of craft are local mackerel luggers. In the foreground, four white painted pilot gigs sit at their moorings, ready for action. Sights such as this were once common around the smaller ports of the UK, and it is not difficult to conjecture just how many people were so employed. Ship building, repairing, storing, crewing and general upkeep would have required a cast of hundreds, just in St.Ives alone!

139. St. Ives in 2007 →

Just a very few fishing boats were sitting on the sand in this spring time photograph. However, the many fine old buildings beyond had looked out over much activity earlier in their existence. Their upkeep has probably been far easier from the tourism income, nevertheless.

140. SS HAYLE at Hayle

From the early 1700s tin and copper smelting processes using imported Welsh coal were established, followed by a foundry in 1779 by John Harvey. This ultimately employed hundreds of men engaged in the manufacture of heavy mining machinery. Starting in 1787 a small fleet of sailing ships would handle coal and pig iron imports and then transport finished machinery away by sea if so required. Ship building at their own yard logically followed - Harveys were in the right business as iron ship construction started taking over from wood. Hayle has always been hampered to some degree by the shallow nature of the estuary, and as steel ship building moved to the North of England and Scotland, the local yard finally closed around 1900. Small colliers for a local power station and tankers for a petroleum depot ceased visiting in the 1970s. Apart from a little ship breaking in that decade, siltation has seriously inhibited ship access. The photograph dates from around 1912 and shows the steam coaster *Hayle* 476g/1893, a local Harvey product. It is thought that she may just have been lengthened in this image, since mainmast and derricks are missing. Other steam coasters and railway wagons fill this busy industrial scene.

141. Hayle in 2007 →

This low water view has just a smattering of small craft lining the shoreline. South Quay is on the left with East Quay in the middle distance. The railway viaduct passes just behind the camera, and there is little today to indicate the once great industrial complex that existed hereabouts.

142. SS MARENA at Portreath →

Previously just a fishing port, Portreath saw development from the mid eighteenth century to expedite local mineral exports. In 1809 a mineral tramway carried copper ore to the new basins allowing ship loading and the movement of coal, in reverse to power the mine machinery. In the photograph from the 1930s the steam coaster *Marena* 303g/1908 lies at anchor waiting to enter port. Her owners were the County of Cornwall Shipping Company, at Portreath. A fairly typical coaster of her day, she has nevertheless, had an extra short sampson post added at the break of the forecastle, to carry the forward derrick. The crew while away the time until high water by engaging in a spot of fishing over the stern. Bain & Co. also ran steamers from here having started with sailing ships before 1870. Portreath was regarded as the harbour for Redruth.

143. Portreath inner basin in 2007

This view is taken from the inner end of Portreath's final harbour layout. Today, homes stand each side of the basins where once vast piles of ore were stockpiled ready for shipment. Suitable only for ships of about 300 tons capacity, the entrance channel to the port was one of the most challenging, especially in sailing ship days. It demanded 'dog-leg' turns under the cliffs and that would have required much warping on ropes and capstans, to gain entrance. The harbour entrance lies off to the right at the end of the basins visible here. The last cargo ships to enter Portreath were mainly small Dutch coasters with coal in the 1960s. They were well suited for the job.

144. Portreath from above →

The far walls of the narrow dock basins can just be picked out above the modern white terraced houses. The 'dog-leg' layout of the entrance channel can clearly be seen, at low water, beneath the towering cliffs. Fine seamanship indeed was required routinely at Portreath, as there was no room for error.

145. Newquay in the 1900s

Ships had traded to nearby Porth and the Gannel for centuries before the development of Newquay. An early pier 'of sorts' gave some protection for small craft before a more substantial version appeared in the late 1500s – hence the name. 1833 saw major improvements, and a branch railway line duly arrived on the scene in 1849, having tunnelled through the cliffs at the back of the harbour. This would greatly expedite mineral ore and china clay exports to the waiting ships. A number of ship owners were based at Newquay whose vessels were engaged in 'cross-trading'- that is, carrying goods between ports elsewhere. Local shipyards turned out ketches and schooners. Trade gradually dwindled over the fifty years before departure of the very last cargo in 1922. In the photograph from the early years of the twentieth century, there is much of interest. The now isolated stone pier in the deeper part of the harbour had been added in 1870, and was rail accessed by way of a wooden trestle style bridge, from the cliff bottom. Two railway sidings permitted direct loading from wagons to ships. A local ketch and some topsail schooners are tied up each side, whilst, a very long way from home, a laden Thames or Medway sailing barge is moored. Their voyaging in the English Channel was common enough, but a trip around Lands End – something much more adventurous! Fish barrels and attendant paraphernalia make up the beach scene.

146. Newquay in 2007

Local fishing boats and pleasure craft now predominate in this once industrial harbour. The isolated stone jetty section is here viewed end-on from the shore having long lost its wooden connecting trestle to the rail tunnel. Today, of course, Newquay thrives from the holiday and leisure industry, with the vital added ingredient of surfing.

↙ 147. ST HELEN PEELE at Padstow

Padstow is believed to date from as early as 513, of monastic origins. The first stone pier was constructed before 1536, and in the 1600s sailing packets were running to Ireland. General trade around the Irish Sea was brisk. Throughout the seventeenth and eighteenth centuries, slate, tin and copper ore were shipped away. Arrival of the railway saw quantities of fresh fish sent to the London markets, and in 1911 some 3,000 tons was so transported by the London & South Western Railway. Shipyards constructed vessels up to about 800 tons in size, and Padstow remained North Cornwall's largest port, despite a difficult entrance and the River Camel's shifting sands. Ships owned at Padstow also spent much of their time trading overseas. In the final years of commercial traffic, cargoes of grain, coal, fertiliser and timber were handled in vessels up to about 1,500 tons. Today, some local sand dredging continues for the building trade. The subject of this photograph is unique. Serious difficulties had often been experienced in sailing ship times in putting the oared lifeboat out to sea during emergencies. The Royal National Lifeboat Institution had built the steam tug *Helen Peele* 133g/1901, especially to be based at Padstow, for the purpose of towing the lifeboat to sea in adverse conditions. She would in fact carry out some rescues herself, and could undertake towage as required. In this photograph she sits on the mooring awaiting the next 'shout', and presumably could raise steam quicker than the average steam tug, when the need arose. She has noticeably more deck accommodation than most tugs, and no doubt would have carried extra life-saving, salvage and towage gear. After her life-saving career was over in 1929, it is believed she converted to a private steam yacht.

148. MARY B. MITCHELL

Some china clay continued to be exported via Padstow from Wenford Bridge by rail. The network of branch lines in this area was particularly hard hit by Dr. Beeching's closure plan, implemented in the 1960s. The line through Wadebridge to Padstow closed in 1966. In the photograph from exactly thirty years earlier, a line of basic open wagons, well tarpaulined, have brought clay to be loaded into the *Mary B.Mitchell* 229g/1892. Carrickfergus built, this fine old three masted schooner, had acted as one of the famous 'Q-ships' during WWI. Quite heavily armed she nevertheless presented the image of a totally innocent merchantman, whilst boldly taking on surfaced submarines, who thought they were about to torpedo her. She was credited with three successes. Returning to normal peacetime trading, she went to Tyrells' of Arklow in the 1930s, and had an auxiliary motor fitted. In 1944 the old ship was caught in a severe gale between Dublin and Silloth, becoming overwhelmed, but the crew were rescued, and she perished on rocks in the Solway Firth.

149.   MV MANNIN

Seen in Padstow in 2006 is the now locally based harbour grab dredger, *Mannin* 172g/1972. Once operated by the Isle of Man Harbour Board, she replaced a steamer of the same type and name. *Mannin* was built at Cooke's Shipyard, Wivenhoe, Essex. Very few harbours now have their own dredgers to keep channels clear, and often contractors are brought in periodically to 'blitz' channels, usually with trailing suction type craft.

150. MV SAND SNIPE (2) →

Awaiting her next foray out to collect sand is the reduced version of the ship in No.29

151.   Padstow's working harbour in 2006 →

Local fishing craft and small boats abound and this scene makes an interesting comparison to No 148, when the jetty was rail connected and china clay exported

152. SS DUNRAVEN at Wadebridge

With its distinctive 1468 dated stone bridge across the River Camel, (built on the revenue from the wool trade), Wadebridge has seen greatly fluctuating fortunes with regard to commercial shipping. Water levels in the River Camel and the shifting nature of the sandbanks have often severely restricted access to the old port, perhaps to just a day or two each side of the fortnightly spring tides. The last major burst of activity seems to have been in the early 1900s, when schooners, ketches and even small steamers percolated up the seven miles of the Camel from Padstow. The photograph dates from around this time and shows the steamer *Dunraven* 261g/1897, departing for the trip back down river to the sea. She was built by Craggs of Middlesbrough and joined the small Bristol Channel fleet of Pocketts, of Swansea, being sold foreign in 1906. They were better known for their excursion paddle steamers around the Bristol Channel up until WWI, but continued cargo services into the 1920s. In the background trading vessels are busily working cargoes just below the bridge on both sides of the river.

153. MV NOVA →

Seen just downstream of the bridge unloading a cargo of fertiliser in 1961, is the German motor coaster *Nova* 234g/1939. The nature of the river bed clearly shows the restriction on shipping, in this low water scene.

154. Wadebridge Town Quay in 2006 →

Taken from much the same spot as No.153, the Town Quay now supports luxury homes in place of the industry of old. Down stream the high level bridge now carries through traffic way above the River Camel, clear of Wadebridge. The central sandbank below the old bridge now supports permanent plant growth, and it may not be too long before trees take hold. Small yachts and craft still manage to navigate the river.

155. Bude Canal and lock

Unlike much of Cornwall, the Bude area was not rich in minerals, and even the agricultural soils were poorish. In 1774, John Edyvean planned to transport lime rich sea sand from Bude inland, to enrich the soil. In a major feat of engineering two canals were constructed, one towards Launceston and the other, Holsworthy. Construction ran from 1819 to 1825 and involved three sets of locks, with no less than six inclined planes along thirty five and a half miles of canal, over difficult terrain. Unique 'tub-boats' carried about four tons apiece in trains of four or six. Horse drawn on the level, their small wheels at each corner permitted travel up and down the tracked, incline planes, where ingenious water powered engineering solutions, and continuous chains raised or lowered the 'train'. In some years up to 50,000 tons of sea sand went inland by this method and it handled other commodities such as coal. Once Bude was reached by the westward thrust of the railways, this amazing system of waterway transport fell into disuse by around 1891. Bude continued as a small commercial port until just before WWII. The harbour entrance through Bude Haven from the sea has always been a challenge for mariners, and although Bude is today a very popular holiday destination, it has not fallen to the 'mass yacht marina syndrome', seen in so many other locations around England's shores. Bude Museum, by the lock gates, houses a brilliant display of the area's once unique tub-boat system.

In the photograph from the early 1900s, a topsail schooner, ketches and trading cutters lay about just inside the lock and out in the Haven, awaiting a rise of tide. A section of trackway is visible by the river outlet on the right.

156. CERES

This remarkable old ship finally foundered off the North Devon coast in 1936, after 125 years of trading. She had been built at Salcombe in 1811 and ran as a fruit smack to Spain early in her career. Of 32 reg.tons, she originally carried about 52 tons of cargo. In 1852 she came under the Bude ownership of the Petherick family, and would thus remain for a further 84 years in service. In 1869, when under repair it was decided to lengthen the ship, so she was literally cut in two and an additional 15ft mid body section built in, thus increasing cargo capacity to 85 tons. With the addition of a mizzen mast she moved from cutter to ketch status. A further upgrade happened in 1912 when her first auxiliary motor was fitted – a 36hp engine – she was already a centenarian! In the latter decades of the nineteenth century she traded as far as London, the Channel Islands, Liverpool and across to Ireland, apart from the usual Bristol Channel haunts. She weathered many a storm, and it is believed must have carried some 250,000 tons of cargo, without loss of a single life! She foundered after springing a leak with a cargo of slag off Baggy Point, North Devon, not far from home.

← 157. MV ARRAN MONARCH

This little vessel started out as an Admiralty victualling steam lighter *VIC 57*, 147g/1946. Built at Faversham, Kent by J.Pollock, she became *Arran Monarch* in 1948, and later ran for some time to Watchet, Somerset for the Wansbrough Paper Company. By 1964 she had become a motor ship, and converted to serve as a sand dredger at Llanelly, under the name *Coedmor*. Tonnage became 181gross. She was still in existence in 2000 working as a sand dredger in North Cornwall. The photograph is believed to be taken at Bude, and as she is still unmistakeably named *Arran Monarch* and has no visible wheelhouse or funnel, it is possible that she was undergoing conversion at the time. Her original appearance would have been the same as No.92.

← 158. Bude Canal in 2004

The lock gate railings can just be made out in the far distance towards the sea. Few boats were moored at this delightfully tranquil spot in the August holiday season.

159. MV DESPATCH

A number of ex-Dutch coasters came to the British flag when owners in Holland started to 'up-size' and upgrade their fleets. Seen here in her earlier years, she still has the hinged mast arrangement enabling passage under low bridges. In the 1970s this useful little ship, without name change, joined Captain Peter Herbert's small fleet owned in Bude. Latterly, *Despatch* 199g/1931 lost her distinctive mast and derricks in deference to the trend for shore craneage for cargo work. The masthead steaming light would then be moved to a simple pole mast on the forecastle head. She finally became the last locally owned ship to trade from Bideford.

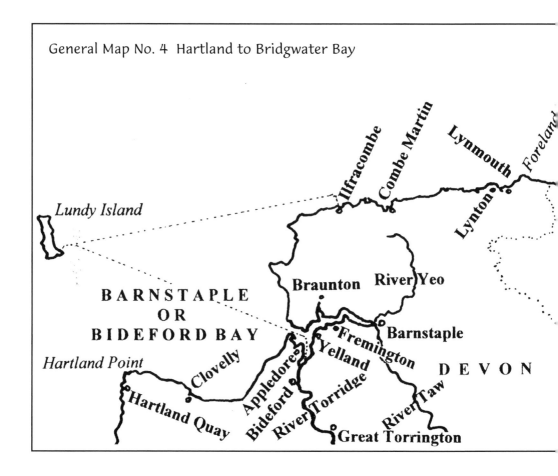

General Map No. 4 Hartland to Bridgwater Bay

Hartland's Traders

Leaving Cornwall at Bude, the Devon coast becomes ever more rugged with towering cliffs and treacherous rock ledges extending out to sea. Inland, long ago, roads were merely irregular trackways especially those serving the Hartland area, which was remote even from the landward side. In pre-industrial days it was therefore not surprising that such goods and commodities that were required by the sparse local populace, would travel by sea. This in itself presented major difficulties, as few indeed were the spots suitable for the small cargo carriers of the day to beach and unload. Most trade of this type took place in the summer months as more clement weather generally prevailed, or at least Atlantic storms arrived less frequently!

Hartland had seen some seaborne trade for hundreds of years before Henry VIII's dissolution of the monasteries. When land ownership restrictions eased in the second half of the 1500s, the only feasible spot for a small, protected harbour construction was chosen – Hartland Quay had arrived. In the decades either side of 1600 a number of similar pier building schemes got underway around the hazardous West Country coasts. Construction techniques were surprisingly advanced, given man power alone, and would make a fascinating study in their own right. We shall now turn to describe the gallant little ships involved, and the cargoes they carried.

In common with much of the beach handled trade around the English coasts at the time, the

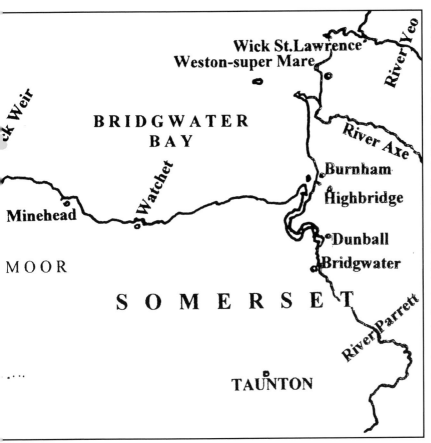

ships were mainly tiny, typically just 30 to 40 reg. tons in size. At Hartland coal from South Wales, limestone for the local kilns (for plaster and mortar), timber, bricks, tiles, slates, and a full range of agricultural and domestic supplies would be brought inwards. Mostly goods came from the nearest large towns of Bideford and Barnstaple, while at harvest time, grain went the other way. The ships were usually single masted, gaff rigged sloops and cutters, all generally referred to as 'smacks'. They had to be of immensely strong construction to withstand not only foul weather, but the constant stresses of sitting aground while loading and unloading, yet, they had to have the ability to remain upright at all times. Cargo work usually involved unloading by a gaff or 'boom' with a simple gin tackle, block and pulley. Horse drawn carts would wait directly alongside to receive coal lifted out in large baskets, and thence 'shot' directly down a chute into the cart. At Hartland these were known as 'butts'.

Of course bad weather could erupt at any time and once afloat the smacks would tend to lurch about like 'bucking broncos'. Extra heavy duty rope, 'springs' would be run out to stout mooring posts in an endeavour to restrain things. The ships built for this local trade had especially large fairlead openings in their transoms and bulwarks, for just such eventualities. The local name for these special heavy moorings in this part of the country seems to have been 'junks'. Some of the smacks were actually owned at Hartland, and their amazing longevity is testament to both their construction and the supreme seamanship of those who handled them.

Serious storms often damaged the pier and not infrequent repair work had to be undertaken. In 1887, a particularly vicious storm demolished much of its outer end, the result of which was the 'writing on the wall' for Hartland's quay. After this date a few more smacks managed to berth in the remains of the harbour, but in 1893 the final cargo came in care of the *Rosamund Jane* 34r/1834, a Padstow built smack. A number of the smacks were owned and crewed by Clovelly men, from just around the corner. By 1896 the remnants of the old pier were spread right across the floor of the old harbour itself. Today, Hartland Quay has a special magic appeal for the modern tourist, and the Museum's fine display of this lost port's sea trade and industry, is essential viewing.

160. Unloading at Hartland

This is the classic view of Hartland Quay with a smack sitting close to the pier for protection at low water. The horses and their 'butts' are alongside and frantic efforts are being made to discharge the cargo as soon as possible. The less valuable commodities would sometimes simply be pitched off the ship into a pile on the harbour bottom for later collection, eg, limestone. The jagged rocks all around, plus the difficulties in bringing in such un-powered craft, can now only be wondered at!

161. Hartland Quay remains in 2006

Looking to the right of where the pier once stood, we can see rubble across the otherwise sandy bottom, which had once been the pier's stonework. Yet, in the 1500s this had been considered the best site for a harbour locally, and after all, it did survive for three hundred years of trade.

162. Hartland Point Lighthouse

Not far north of the Quay lies Hartland Point which marks an important course alteration for ships coming into the Bristol Channel ports. Shipping passes between the point and Lundy Island, a few miles to the westward. Hartland Point headland reaches some 350ft in height

and often suffers from mist, fog or low cloud, so in 1874 the present lighthouse structure was built low down just to avoid such problems. Lundy Island's old North Light had also been subject to visibility problems. The Island shows up well in this 2006 photograph, as does one of the world's newer forms of maritime conveyance – a large car carrier outward bound from the Bristol Channel. Apart from floating, no comparison can sensibly be made with a trading smack!

163. MV FARRINGAY

This rather angular little motor coaster still bears a close resemblance to the form in which she was built as *Empire Farringay* 462g/1944, at Goole, Yorkshire. A series of these ships were constructed of straight plates and angular sections during WWII. By this method and in time of great shortages, in-experienced steel workers could manufacture sections away from the shipyards. The whole would then be finally assembled at a yard. Some forty ships emerged as '*Chants*' – generally taken as Admiralty code for 'channel tankers', whilst a further twenty five came out as dry cargo ships. Many of both types traded long after WWII in the commercial world. The example in this photograph traded for J.H.K.Griffin, of Cardiff, and was one of the last around the United Kingdom. Welsh coal for Bideford Gasworks was a good example of cargo carried during the 1950s. Even as late as 1979 the ship found new owners under the Panamanian flag.

→ 164. Clovelly in the 1900s

The present stone pier has existed since at least 1597, when completed by George Carey as part of a general expansion at Clovelly, above and below the cliff. Although primarily a fishing harbour, locally owned trading smacks also served other remote communities around the Hartland area. Seafaring was therefore an important employer, and as Clovelly offered the nearest thing to proper shelter on this rugged coast, it was popular. In the event of a blow from the north, a dash to the lee of Lundy Island could be made. In this 1900s study, a couple of the tall masted sailing trawlers are drawn up to the beach, and far right, one can just make out a larger trading smack.

→ 165. Clovelly in 2006

This is a similar view from the pier about a century later, and small boats and fishing craft abound. Ground chains run from the shore to the pier to give secure moorings for the boats as they lift and drop on the big tidal range here. The buildings around the arch look little altered, but the roofline of the Red Lion Hotel has certainly become more uniform in height.

↙ 166. Clovelly Pier

The view northwards from a little way up the cliff path shows the solid structure of the pier. Large rocks were used to form the base, decreasing in size with height. Stone steps incut, allow access down to the boats or harbour floor at low water. Stout vertical rubbing timbers act as boat fenders. This type of pier construction appeared at a number of West Country minor harbours, thus turning a simple exposed landing site into a useful facility. At Clovelly, the Victorians were quick to recognise the full potential of tourism, and paddle steamers became regular callers, weather permitting on their runs from South Wales and the Bristol area. Clovelly, would sometimes be included on the Ilfracombe - Lundy Island trip. Local boatmen brought passengers ashore in their small boats whilst the steamers lay as close as possible off-shore. Such trips, by Campbell's white funnelled paddle steamers ceased in the 1960s, as the general public found motoring and overseas holidays increasingly more to its liking. In the 2006 photograph, a black cat on the wall appeared oblivious to the sheer drop beyond, and frequent fuss from passers-by!

167. Appledore Quayside

Situated close to the confluence of the Rivers Taw (Barnstaple), and Torridge (Bideford), there has been a port here since monastic beginnings in the 1300s. Queen Elizabeth I granted 'freeport' status in 1588, since the place provided so many ships and men to fight the Spanish Armada. In the eighteenth century Appledore was a main tobacco importing centre. By 1845 a continuous quayside replaced existing wharves and back gardens. The quay was rebuilt in 1997. Ship building has been important for many centuries and in the latter days of wooden hulled ship construction, many workers emigrated to Prince Edward Island (P.E.I.) in Canada, continuing to build brigantines and schooners for British owners. Timber was plentiful on P.E.I. and stocks considerably reduced at home. The shipyards of Robert Cock, P.K.Harris and J. Hinks were eventually all superceded by Appledore Shipbuilders Ltd in 1963, and their output to the end of the century was both varied and prolific. Dredgers, tugs, rig support ships, ferries, gas tankers and container ships up to several thousand tons capacity, were all floated out of the large covered building dock. Sadly, as with all similar shipyards in Britain, fierce competition from overseas, and particularly from Far Eastern yards, has seen orders dry up in recent years. In the 1930s photograph a couple of local ketches lie furthest away, whilst two river barges are moored centrally, one of which still carries sail. Clinker built boats fill in the foreground. During the depression years, the deeper parts of the estuary were used as in South Devon harbours for the lay-up of out of work merchant ships. Some 15-16 vessels in the 2,000 to 7,000 gross ton range were present at the peak, in the Appledore / Bideford area.

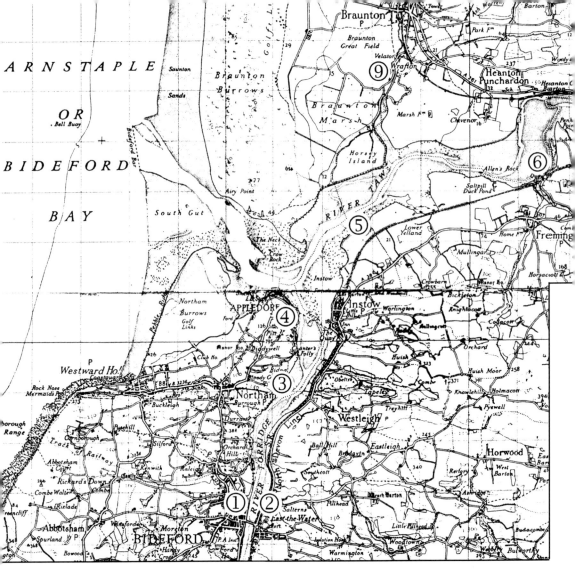

Local Map No. 9
River Torridge to River Taw

(1) Bideford Quay
(2) East-the-Water
(3) Appledore Shipyard
(4) Appledore Quay
(5) Yelland Jetties
(6) Fremington Quay
(7) Taw Bridge (newly opened in 2007)
(8) River Yeo Quays, Barnstaple
(9) Braunton Pill

168. NONSUCH

J. Hinks built many ships over a century, but latterly the firm became specialists in the construction of replica wooden hulled sailing ships, completed to a very high standard indeed. A Viking Longship, a *Golden Hinde*, and the *Nonsuch* were excellent examples. This last vessel was launched in 1968 ready for the 300th anniversary commemoration of the incorporation of the Hudsons Bay Company in 1970. The original *Nonsuch* had been built in 1650 at Wivenhoe, Essex and was a mere 36ft. long at the waterline. She measured just 43 tons burden and successfully sailed to Canada in 1668, trading whilst there, and returning to London in 1669. A monumental achievement for so small a craft – she was no larger than those Hartland smacks!

169. MV SAND DART

This smart little sand suction dredger 499g/1957 came from the P.K Harris yard at Appledore. She joined a fleet of similarly employed vessels working along the South Coast to provide sand and ballast for the growing building industry. All of South Coast Shipping's earlier ships had been converts from dry cargo coasters. This aerial view clearly shows the long suction dredging pipe stowed on deck. The cargo is pumped directly into the single hold until sand has displaced the seawater. En route to port the last 'drainings' can be seen running from the scuppers. These ships all relied upon shore cranes for discharging the cargo. *Sand Dart* had diesel electric propulsion and later traded as *Pen Dart*.

170. MV ARCO DART
Some thirty years later and dredging technology has moved on considerably. *Arco Dart* 1,309g/1990 has the bridge and accommodation in the forepart of the vessel. Larger dredging pipes are situated on the starboard side, but the main change has been the provision of full self-discharging equipment. With a travelling grab gantry, plus conveyors, unloading to any suitable clear quayside is now possible. This of course eliminates the shore crane and speeds cargo discharge. *Arco Dart* makes regular landings of ballast at Appledore today.

171. MV TORRIDGE LASS
In the 1950s, this WWII built ship was trading for Torridge Coasters of Bideford. *Torridge Lass* 411g/1944 had been launched as *Empire Fabric* at Henry Scarr's, Hessle Shipyard. She is another in the series described in No.163, but in this case the forehatch has not been raised. Two feet longer in construction and she would have required a second masthead steaming light (150ft). In 1969 she went to Canada for further trading.

172. Bideford Quay around 1900

An important town in Saxon times, it became increasingly so in the early days of trade with America, especially Virginia and Maryland. In the 1700s Newfoundland became a major market with wool a key export. In the early 1700s Bideford ships brought back more tobacco than any other port except London, for the local merchants. The fine stone arch bridge across the River Torridge dates from the 1500s, and its uneven sized arches are believed to reflect how much local merchants were able to afford each, towards its construction. The first recorded quay dates from 1619 and the present long quay from around 1890. In 1835 across the Torridge at East-the-Water, a gas works served by colliers from South Wales, began generating. In the 1930s trade consisted of coal, timber and fertiliser imports, with some ball clay exported. The large tidal range permitted ships of up to about 1,500 tons capacity to trade to the port, which mostly dries out at each low water. Today, with the design of modern motor coasters it is possible over spring tide periods to load ships up to about 3,000 tons, and cargoes of ball clay are exported regularly. The Lundy Island Company have their main headquarters here on the quayside, and between Easter and October the supply ship takes visitors on the two hour trip to the Island. Ilfracombe is the alternative base when tides rise insufficiently at Bideford. In the 1900 photograph, a heavily built Baltic timber schooner is riding high, ready for sea.

173. SS ROMA

With the long straight Bideford Quay entirely to herself, *Roma* 181g/1903 is evidently not quite afloat. She had spent some fifty years in the coastal trades having been built at Larne, then rebuilt at Belfast in 1913. She was powered by a 32hp steam engine and during the 1930s ran for the Straits Steamship Company of Liverpool, surviving well into the 1950s.

174. MV ALDERD L.

The two coasters visible here typify the 1960s period. Most such vessels still had a pair of cargo derricks, yet they were to be increasingly seen simply swung out of the way in port, whilst mobile quay cranes did the job. *Alderd L.* 384g/1955 could carry about 480 tons of cargo, and she was just one member of a large collective management fleet. The Dutch firm of Wijnne & Barends were merely one such firm so specialising. Netherlands' built ships could always be distinguished by the 'acorn' finial at the mast top.

175. MV ALEXANDER KUPRIN

This 2003 photograph well illustrates the absence of water at low tide in Bideford. The large motor coaster with the off-set funnel is the Russian *Alexander Kuprin* 2,319g/ 3,030d/1996. One of a standard class of ships (there are numerous), she shows just what size cargo can be lifted on a shallow draught of scarcely 15ft With an overall length of just under 300ft, this is about the maximum possible for Bideford, and the ship has been turned to face down stream while in ballast, to simplify departure when loaded. Just visible beneath the right arch of Bideford's by-pass bridge can be seen the distant Appledore Shipyard Buildings.

176.   KATHLEEN & MAY

Looking resplendent at her home berth of East-the-Water is the schooner *Kathleen & May* 138g/1900, and originally the topsail schooner *Lizzie May*. She came from a shipyard at Connah's Quay on the River Dee in North Wales. Her long association with Bideford started in 1913 when registered in the port. During the1930s she was running for Thomas Jewell of Appledore, and an 80hp engine had been fitted. She continued in coastal trade until around 1960. Your Author remembers looking over the old ship in 1965 when she was in lay-up at Marchwood, Southampton. At that time a large sea-valve had been installed at the bottom of the hold in readiness to scuttle the poor old ship for the making of some epic film! Mercifully, this indignity never materialised. Later she would be open to the public on the Thames and subsequently reached Gloucester Docks, in poor order. In 1998 her fortunes and prospects greatly improved when purchased by Bideford business man, Steve Clarke. On arrival at Bideford the ship was craned out of the water onto the quayside where a mammoth rebuilding programme got underway. Many timber frames and planks were replaced and the ship re-rigged and re-engined. Re-launched in the summer of 2001, she made a voyage to Youghal in Eire. Today, the ship is open to the public at East-the-Water at certain times, and is well worth a visit.

The Bideford, Westward Ho! & Appledore Railway is illustrated on pages 152-155

177. From East-the-Water

Looking across the Torridge in 2003 we see in the foreground the decaying remains of one of the once common river barges. Such craft worked all around the Taw and Torridge estuary, and well into the rivers. This example, although totally waterlogged has not yet quite fallen asunder, and the central hatchway is still intact. When collecting sand from banks in the estuary, craft of this type would be put aground as the tide receded. The 'gang' would then shovel like fury until the barge was deemed to be laden thence flotation would hopefully occur as the tide rose, for the trip home. Beyond lies moored the Dutch coaster *Silmaril* 1,399g/1985 loading export ball clay. Over to the right is the Lundy Company ship, described in Nos. 180 and 181.

178. MT ST. MAWES →

Now privately owned, this classic harbour tug began work on the River Thames as a member of William Watkins fleet as *Ionia* 187g/1960. Later she moved to the Falmouth Towage Company and was a successor to the steam tug *St.Mawes* described in No.114. Bideford's unevenly arched bridge can be seen beyond.

179. MV CELTIC VOYAGER →

When photographed at Bideford in 2006 this vessel had not long since joined the Welsh controlled fleet of Charles M. Willie & Co. The attractive funnel emblem perfectly displays this association. Modern motor coasters may seem rather 'boxy' in design but nevertheless they are most efficient. *Celtic Voyager* 1,957g/1985 sails under the Bahamas flag and registry, and is clearly showing her I.M.O. recognition number. This additional requirement for international trading vessels came in during recent years to help deter and detect cargo and ship fraud, a major problem in a few areas of the world. Ahead of this ship another of similar size is also loading, but she has the 'retractable' type of wheelhouse. *Grace* 1,599g/2005.

180. MV OLDENBURG

Just about to 'swallow' two empty rubbish skips for Lundy Island, loaded by her own hydraulic deck crane, the day passengers for the 10.00 sailing from Bideford are already aboard. *Oldenburg* 313g/1958 was Bremen built, and ran in German waters for many years before coming to the Lundy service. She is well suited to the job being substantially built and of twin engined, twin propeller design. The Devon flag flies proudly from the port yard arm, in September 2006.

181. Lundy bound →

It was rather a dull but calm day, as the vital Lundy crossing gets underway, with a very good number of day visitors onboard. In accordance with the expected rise of tide on the River Torridge, the passengers may well find themselves disembarking at Ilfracombe in the evening. Their journey back to Bideford would then be completed by motor coach.

182. MV ROELOF JAN at Yelland →

In the early 1950s, a coal fired power station came into service at Yelland. It would be supplied with coal by coasters berthing at its own jetty. Generally, these ships were in the 800-1,000 ton capacity range. In the photograph the Dutch flag *Roelof Jan* 500g/820d/1957 is under the gantry grab. Hopper fed conveyors then carried the coal to the stockpiles. The photograph dates from 1969, and it is believed that this ship was also the last to load, at nearby Fremington Quay in the same year. An oil depot jetty at Yelland closed as recently as 2006.

183.   SS MARI ELI at Fremington

As the River Taw's shallow sandy nature began to debar most shipping from Barnstaple, the Taw Valley Railway and Dock Company opened their facility at Fremington, where larger ships could more regularly dock. Clay shipments of up to 1,000 tons were regular, and at the peak some 50,000 tons of coal passed inwards over the quay, annually. Also, Baltic timber cargoes were handled, most commodities travelling to and from the wharves by rail wagons. The closure of the Barnstaple-Bideford-Torrington railway line in 1969 brought an end to Fremington Quay's trade. Today, a long distance footpath and cycleway follows the course of the old railway line, and is very popular with its scenic views of the local rivers and estuary. At the site of the old Fremington Station, a small but informative heritage centre is worth a visit. In the photograph probably dating from the late 1930s, the Spanish veteran *Mari Eli* 1,080g/1897 had just loaded what was believed to be a record cargo of clay for the port, 1,300 tons. She came from a Greenock shipyard, and under her 8th name of *Punta Almina,* was still in the registers in 1959.

184.   MV RIVER AVOCA →

The steam cranes are hard at work on the quay in this 1960s image loading clay for the Eire potteries into the holds of the *River Avoca,* 384g/1948. Until 1963 this ship carried the name *Stevonia,* but then joined the fleet of Hall & Tyrell at Arklow, Eire. The busy wharf had but a few more years in trade.

185.   Fremington Quay in 2007 →

Today, this is a pleasant grassy spot indeed, and the long distance 'Tarka' trail curves away to the right behind the camera en route to Yelland, Instow and Bideford. The industrial clutter has vanished although the signal box and parts of the station platform remain. The protruding central part of the quay, best visible in No.183, lies behind the next subject described in No.186. Evidently much further silting has occurred since the days of cargo shipping.

186. MV SEVERN SANDS

This un-remarkable little sand suction dredger has somehow managed to outlive her contemporaries, although she has now been out of trade since 2005. Built in Holland as *Isca,* 550g/676d/1960 she worked in the Bristol Channel area, until sold to France in 1977. Under the names of *Le Ferlas,* thence *Ferlas* she continued trading there until a surprise move back to Newport, South Wales in 1995, when she acquired her present name, and resumed local dredging work. She moved to the River Taw in 2006 and at present awaits her fate.

187. Rolle Quay, Barnstaple →

Trade is known to have taken place at Barnstaple in the 1200s and it certainly flourished in Elizabethan times to around 1600, with wool a major export item. As previously mentioned, the River Taw's extremely shallow nature has always tended to frustrate regular shipping movements here. In the 1930s it was stated that just five ships up to about 350 tons apiece could berth, but then only over spring tides. Castle Quay remained in-accessible at neap tides. In 1899 Stanbury and Sons, corn merchants opened their large mill premises on Rolle Quay. This backwater is actually on a Taw tributary, the River Yeo. A reasonable depth of water here made the wharves busy with small coasters and local barges, and in 1929 some 100,000 tons of grain, coal, timber and manure were handled. Much of the cargo received came up in barges from steamers anchored in Appledore Pool. Recent years have seen waterborne trade to Barnstaple cease, as further river shallowing has occurred. A new high level by-pass road bridge just below the town should solve much of Barnstaple's

road traffic woes- (this opened in summer 2007). In the 1920s photograph, three little steamers are moored by the Mill in the River Yeo at Rolle Quay, and are believed to be- *Parrett* 129g/1915 owned in Bridgwater, *Roma* 181g/1903, and *Devonia* 98g/1894 owned in Bideford.

188.   MV STAN WOOLAWAY

W.Woolaway & Sons Ltd., of Barnstaple, brought this smart little ship into service in 1955. Dutch built, she has a full set of hatch covers and tarpaulin, and therefore would have suited cargo other than sand or ballast. The dredging pipe can be seen stowed, and the extra large number of scupper outlets in the bulwarks, certainly indicate suitability for dredging sand cargoes. A very light laden draught of just 7ft 9.5in on a gross tonnage of only 278, would surely permit access to Barnstaple. The ship appears brand new in the photograph – ships in such trades do not normally stay quite so pristine.

189. The new Taw Bridge (2006)

In the foreground lies the old Severn motor barge *Deerhurst* 158g/1933 still showing her Gloucester registry. In recent times she had been operating locally for the West Country Sand & Gravel Company, but is now out of trade. Beyond, the A39 Barnstaple 'by-pass' bridge is rapidly taking shape across the Taw. A temporary lift bridge is in place during construction.

190. Barnstaple waterfront in 2007 →

Barnstaple's stone bridge across the River Taw is visible far right above the sand bank, in this reverse view to No.189. New buildings have risen around the old Barnstaple Town railway station, and commercial area of Castle Quay. Wooden ship building once took place on the opposite bank. The nearer pile fendering and footbridge on the left mark the entrance to the River Yeo, leading to where the steamers were berthed in No.187.

191. River Yeo quays in 2006 →

Large blocks of apartments now stand approximately where Stanbury & Sons 1899 built mill premises once prospered (No.187). Small craft now sit in their own mud berths where the steamers worked cargo. This photograph is taken from the footbridge over the River Yeo's mouth.

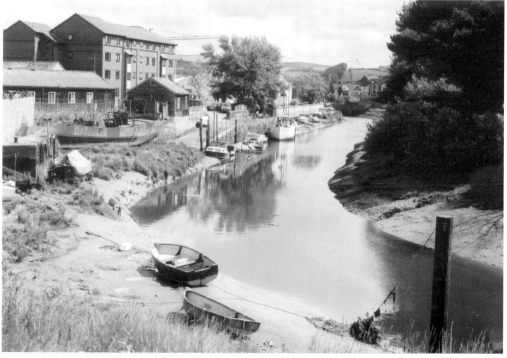

192. Brunswick Wharf

Rolle Quay ends on the left whilst an out-of-work crane used for sand barges sits opposite on Brunswick Wharf. Beyond, the in-evitable juggernaut truck trundles over the bridge as if to emphasise that road transport is now king, to the detriment of all small waterborne cargoes. This area of Barnstaple is now witnessing considerable regeneration.

193. Velator Quay, Braunton →

This isolated quay was constructed in 1853 after some straightening and deepening of the River Caen. It would allow access for ships up to around 130 tons capacity with trade consisting of coal, bricks, fertiliser, and slag imports. Some iron ore from mines above Braunton plus agricultural cargoes made up the export tonnage. Local lime burning was also a significant process. The local arrival of the railway made little difference and Velator Quay continued in trade until the 1950s. This place remained home for a few of the old West Country ketches and schooners, until they finally gave up trading. The town of Braunton can be seen in the background.

194. CLARA MAY →

This photograph in Braunton Pill is included to represent just one of the many such craft once owned in the town. *Clara May* 52r/1891 was built at Plymouth, and by the 1930s ran for Alfred Parkhouse of Braunton. She has already been given a wheelhouse below the mizzen boom, and fitted with a 50hp auxiliary engine (pre1933). The photograph may date from just after WWII.

195. Ilfracombe pre 1900

In sailing ship days, Ilfracombe had trade with North America, the Continent and coastwise, plus some ship building. Steam packets began running to Bristol and other large Bristol Channel ports in the early 1800s, carrying goods and people. The pier extension dating from 1873, would witness the arrival of thousands of day trippers, with on occasion half a dozen paddle steamers tied up abreast. There would be more waiting off shore. Even commercial steam tugs joined in the bonanza, so popular were excursions in the Victorian years. No doubt the activity brought in a little revenue when ship towage or salvage jobs were a bit thin. Ilfracombe's coal supplies came for discharge in the inner harbour, by way of some tiny steamers such as *Agra*, *Velocity* and the long lived *Snowflake*, (see No.197). Today, some fishing, yachting and the Lundy Island service shared with Bideford, are the main activities. In the photograph from about the year 1900, Campbell's paddler *Britannia* 459g/1896 is manoeuvring off the pier, whilst Pockett's *Brighton* 581g/1878 awaits the berth. This ship had previously been on the London Brighton and South Coast Railway's Newhaven to Dieppe run.

196. KATE at Ilfracombe →

The vessel drying her topsail in this atmospheric pre-1900 image is the Appledore built ketch *Kate* 48r/1862. On her starboard side lie two of the trading smack types described particularly in the Hartland notes. The one on the left may well be the local smack, *Diligence* 34r/1803, registered in Barnstaple but owned in Ilfracombe. All of these old timers show just how 'round' or 'blunt' ships' bows were in the early to mid 1800s. Speed would not have been a factor much considered at the time, in coastal trades.

197. SS SNOWFLAKE →

This tiny steamer 90g/1893 had been built to Scottish 'puffer' dimensions as *Maid of Lorn*. She came south to Barnstaple registry in 1897, and a long association with the port of Ilfracombe started. At just 66ft by 18ft length and breadth, her 20hp steam engine must have propelled thousands of tons of coal across the Bristol Channel to Ilfracombe. She survived until WWII, owned in Combe Martin by John Irwin. In the photograph, date unknown, the ship sits in her customary berth in the harbour, and a large wicker basket for lifting coal out of the hold, can be seen on the foredeck. Much of the coal landed along the coasts of North Cornwall, Devon and Somerset, came from Barry in South Wales, or Lydney in Gloucestershire. This latter port specialised in loading the smaller colliers of the day.

198. Ilfracombe Harbour

Here, in a 1930s view across the harbour, *Snowflake* is there just ahead of a larger unidentified steamer. A solitary ketch sits in the middle and just a few boats are present. No motor vehicles are visible at all.

199. Schooners in port

This photograph possibly dates from the late 1940s and two of the diminishing band of three masted schooners, are in port. The nearest ship is the legendary *Result* 122g/1893, steel hulled and built at Carrickfergus, Northern Ireland. Originally rigged as a topsail schooner, she had an auxiliary motor fitted as early as 1914, thence coming to the Barnstaple registry. Requisitioned by the Admiralty, she operated for a time as a 'Q-ship', engaging and damaging a submarine in WWI. Later in another encounter she was on the receiving end, and suffered some damage being duly returned to trade in 1917. In the 1930s she ran for George G. Clarke of Braunton. Over the ensuing years, the schooner rig was gradually cut down in stages to finally, ketch status. Hatchway modification, and installation of a larger engine enabled the ship to compete successfully with more modern tonnage until the late 1960s. Upon withdrawal from trade about 1967, she became an exhibit at the (now defunct) Exeter Maritime Museum. In 1970 she went back to Ireland for preservation, and had the indignity of travelling by low loader truck, to her final resting place at the Ulster Folk and Transport Museum, where she remains to this day.

200.   Ilfracombe inner harbour, 2006

This is a comparison view to No.198 of some seventy years earlier, and ranks of yachts plus a few fishing boats now occupy the harbour. A new concrete slipway leads into the corner so long frequented by *Snowflake,* and this serves the fine new lifeboat house, for the Ilfracombe Station. The sandy bottom hereabouts must be of firm stuff, since close examination reveals several cars 'moored' undoubtedly next to their owners' boats. Now then, what time is high water?

201. SS DEVONIA at Combe Martin

Situated at the seaward end of a blind valley, leading in from the coast, this 'beach' port had long owned trading vessels, being active as early as the 1200s. Some vessels were built here in the 1800s, and today's calm tourist orientated scene is a far cry from the industrial past. Silver and lead smelting works, limestone quarries and kilns, rope making from locally grown hemp, were all significant employers. In the early 1900s the high fields above the harbour produced strawberries in quantity for shipment to South Wales, in season. One can only assume that all traces of coal dust in ships' holds were meticulously removed for such a delicate return 'freight'! Small trading ships continued to be owned in Combe Martin up until WWII, and unlike the more western exposed beach ports, trade went on here, all year round. In the photograph from the 1900s, the little steamer *Devonia* 98g/1894, is moored close to a couple of trading ketches. The strawberry fields mentioned were up on the hill side above the ketches' masts.

202. Combe Martin in 2006

The scene is now one of total tranquillity. It is quite difficult to imagine the activity involved in loading and unloading ships on the beach. As soon as the tide permitted, horses and carts would clatter to and fro, endeavouring to complete the job before the incoming tide or bad weather intervened. This view is taken from the inner end of the Combe Martin inlet.

203. THREE SISTERS at Lynmouth

Lynmouth, with its high level 'twin' Lynton has seen seaborne trade for centuries. The boulder strewn Lyn River rises steeply inland right from the beach, and therefore ships could never enter. The smacks and ketches would come up the channel from the sea to a point just inside the breakwater, to beach and work cargo. This kind of activity largely finished by around WWI, as more suitable ports developed and insurance premiums rose. Ships were just growing ever larger. Local boatmen here, as in Clovelly, would land excursion passengers from the paddle steamers lying offshore when on the Bristol to Ilfracombe run. In this remarkable image from 1914, two little vessels are beached at Lynmouth just out of the main river flow. The *Three Sisters* 42r/1800 came from a Plymouth shipyard, and latterly was owned in Bideford. She must have been a strong contender in longevity terms to the *Ceres,* No.156. Also visible is the even tinier sloop *Melbourne* 14r/1865, registered at Bristol, but owned in Combe Martin.

204. Lynmouth in 2005

Following Lynmouth's August 1952 flooding tragedy, a new stone retaining wall would direct large volumes of descending river water straight out to sea. This is sited about where the little ships were beached in No.203. The photograph shows just how tricky the entrance channel would have been in non-powered shipping days. Yet local knowledge of weather and tide patterns plus fine seamanship ensured relatively few mishaps.

205. A ketch at Porlock Weir

Our first port of call in Somerset is Porlock Weir. It is one of those rare places where nature actually lent a hand towards developing a harbour. An extending pebble and shingle bank out from the shore enabled a small harbour to be established to meet the needs of this very remote community. A lagoon grew behind the protective bank, under the cliffs enabling a set of gates to be established at right angles to the channel from the sea, in the early nineteenth century. In the photograph from about one hundred years later, a ketch lies within the lagoon. Once the gates are closed she can remain afloat whilst working cargo at the wharf, as the tide rushes out. The last cargo brought into Porlock Weir arrived in 1950.

206.   Porlock Weir in 2006
The barrier gates remain open now, so all the small craft based in the lagoon sit aground at low water. A footbridge crosses the entrance by the gates.

207.   The channel to the sea
Depth of water here was certainly not a problem in trading days as ships up to as much as 14ft draught could remain afloat in the lagoon. However, a ninety degree turn had to be executed in front of the gates on arrival, or departure to the sea. This would be achieved by warping the ship on her own ropes. The manoeuvre probably restricted visiting ships to about 100ft in length.

208. Minehead Harbour

Another beach port to benefit from the commercial freedoms of around 1600, Minehead's stone pier opened in 1616. Built of extra large stones, it would be further strengthened in 1682. Local trading ships could enter or leave within two and a half hours of high water, sitting safely on the bottom to work their cargoes. Some ketches were still locally owned in the 1920s and 1930s, and this port too, would see thousands of adventurous trippers arrive on the paddlers. By the 1960s this method of mass people movement had ended, and paddle steamer trips were sadly deemed to be 'old hat'. Coastal cargo trade ceased here about a decade or so later.

209. SS CORBEIL

Seen probably in the 1920s unloading a cargo of sand at Minehead, is the little Bristol owned steamer *Corbeil* 149g/1890. Of iron hulled construction at South Shields, she came to Bristol registry in 1903, and would work for the Bristol Sand & Gravel Company Ltd. In the photograph her single derrick is swung out of the way, and cargo is being placed directly onto a Scammel type lorry by a steam crane.

210. The harbour arm in 2006
Some eighty years have elapsed since the No.209 image and today, the profile of the buildings around the harbour is little altered. The Harbour Café now stands roughly where the old char-a-banc was parked beyond the ship's outswung derrick.

211. SS HORNO at Watchet
The discovery of iron ore in the Brendon Hills led to its subsequent extraction, rail movement to Watchet and thence shipment to South Wales. Loads of around 500 tons seem to have commenced about 1858, and in 1877 a total of 46,000 tons departed. Iron ore discoveries overseas would sound the ultimate death knell for the Watchet operation, although a revival early in the twentieth century met with little success, and closure followed in 1909. The harbour saw a re-build in 1904, and despite the fact that the sea retreats half a mile out at low water, the large rise in tide would enable ships up to 2,000-3,000 tons to enter. →

212. SS BITRALAND and SS KAREN

With piles of esparto grass laying about on the quayside, the driver and fireman of GWR goods engine No.2229 would want to be very careful, as flying sparks could easily start a conflagration. This commodity, often shipped from North African ports, was an essential ingredient, together with woodpulp in paper manufacturing. It was by no means unknown for spontaneous combustion to start in ships' holds so loaded, leading to total loss. As with the railway engine here, ships boilers could send out sparks if coal fired, and deck cargoes of esparto grass were common, as it was such a light material. The nearest steamer is the Swedish *Bitraland* 1,182g/1910, she continued on into the 1960s. Beyond lies the Danish steamer *Karen* 1,293g/1917, and this ship ran for the old firm of Marius Nielsen & Son. Veteran steamers such as these could still find much employment in the timber and associated trades around Northern Europe and the Mediterranean, right into the 1960s. A speed of 9-10 kts was quite adequate, although most had been updated from coal, to oil firing of boilers. The photograph dates from 1954.

← Cargo ships berthed at the East and Railway Quays with much traffic directed to the nearby Wansbrough Paper Company, who required coal, esparto grass and woodpulp for the process. Some general cargo and forest products were also handled, and in 1981 total imports were 133,000 tons. In 1992, the port closed to commercial shipping. In the years 2000-2001, major infrastructure works were undertaken allowing for an 'afloat at all times' yacht marina, in the eastern part of the harbour. This was achieved by new inner piers together with an entrance 'sill' arrangement, so as to maintain water depth for the yacht moorings. There is still something unashamedly nostalgic about this place, as the West Somerset Railway steam trains frequently call at Watchet Station, immediately behind the harbour, on their way to and from Minehead. The photograph, from the early 1950s shows the Swedish veteran steamer *Horno* 1,493g/2,300d/1916 unloading at the East Quay. She had a further decade to trade, and was already on her 6th name. The nearby Dutch coaster *Mercator* 298g/1952 had brought a cargo of potatoes. Two years later she was renamed *Lauwersborg*.

213. Watchet Marina entrance in 2006

Viewed from the outer breakwater, this image shows the entrance to the new
'floating' yacht marina in the eastern part of the harbour. The location of the 'sill'
arrangement can be seen in line with the ex- Naval Fleet tender, moored within.
The crane marks where the cargo ships were docked in No.212. Watchet Station
is just off to the right along the grassy embankment, below the houses.

Local Map No.10 →

(1) Bridgwater Dock
(2) Dunball Wharf
(3) Combwich

214. P1041 and MV PERSEVERANCE

This sunny scene was taken in the corner of the new yacht marina in July 2006. In the foreground is the
Watchet Harbour Board's workboat / hopper barge *Perseverance*, whilst at the foot of the pontoon access, is
the Portsmouth built MGB/MTB, *Gay Archer*, otherwise known as P1041. One of a number of similar craft,
she had been a houseboat on completion of her Navy days, but since, has been fully restored as a floating
memorial to wartime crews.

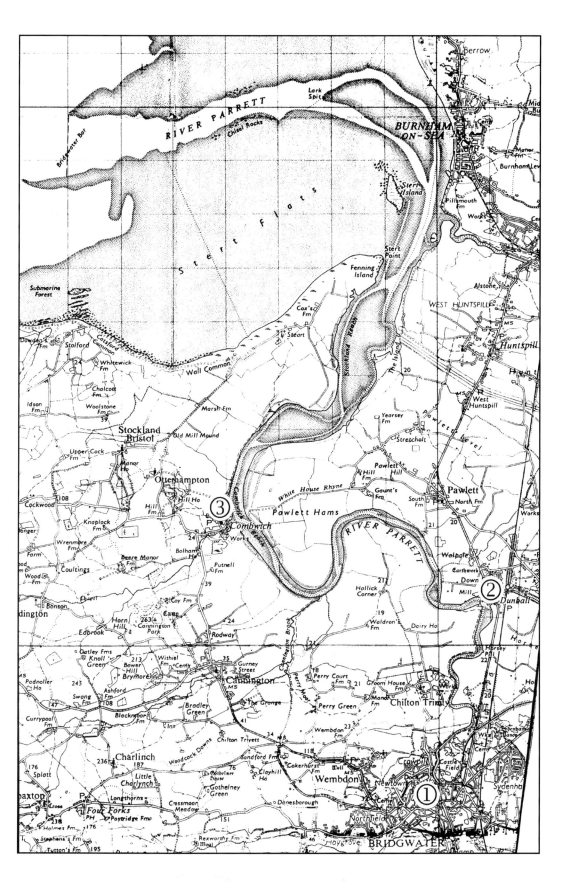

215. IRENE

Our next port of call is Bridgwater on the River Parrett. Beforehand though, it seems singularly appropriate to include this photograph dating from 1959. The subject, the ketch *Irene* 67r/1907, was the last sailing cargo ship to be built at Bridgwater in the shipyard on the banks of the Parrett. Launched amid much ceremony the ketch would continue in trade until about 1960. In the 1930s she was running for the Bridgwater firm of Colthurst, Symons and Company, and a 40hp auxiliary engine installed. Seen in the photograph nearing the end of her trading days, *Irene* is plugging into the swell under mainsail and engine, off Nash Point, South Wales. Once out of trade she made the transition to private yacht, and had various periods of activity and static roles, one of which was based on the upper Thames. Now a centenarian, she survives to this day.

216. Bridgwater Dock in the 1950s

Trading ships had come up the ten miles or so from the sea to Bridgwater's river side wharves for centuries. Ship owning was important to the Town and its ships voyaged to Europe, the Baltic, North America and India, although much local trade passed through the Bristol Channel ports, undertaken by such craft as the *Irene*, and small steamers. A network of canals and improved river navigations enabled goods to be trans-shipped to and from Bridgwater's hinterland. In 1853, some 60,000 tons of goods passed through the inland wharves at Langport, with lesser tonnages moving further inland to Westport and Ilchester. The river barges were of clinker construction, and could carry about 20 tons upstream of Bridgwater. A few continued to work until the early years of the twentieth century. To greatly enhance facilities and enable ships to stay afloat at all times, in 1841 a 3.75 acre dock was built leading off the River Parrett, a short distance downstream from Bridgwater's famous bridge. This had always been the limit for high masted vessels. The dock soon became rail connected under the ownership of the Great Western Railway. Some 2,155 ft of quays were provided and large warehouses on three sides. From the inner end, the Taunton Canal joined the dock by way of a lock. Bridgwater Dock could accommodate a number of coasters up to around 500 tons capacity, access to and from the River Parrett being by a single pair of outer gates and a large basin. A smaller double gated barge lock exists alongside the ship entrance, which has been 'concreted off' from the river. The port was always restricted to the twice daily high tide reaching up the River Parrett. Today,

the dock has become a centre for inland boating on the Bridgwater and Taunton Canal. In the photograph from the 1950s there is much activity with coasters handling cargo. In the foreground F.A.Ashmead's Bristol based, *Peter Leigh* 320g/1941 is moored. The other identifiable vessel is the Dutch coaster *Willem Barendsz* 400g/1940. Timber is being unloaded from the middle ship by shore crane.

217. 'New homes' in 2007

This image makes an interesting comparison with the industrial activity days of No.216. Although taken from the same spot but at a different height, the conversion of the brick built warehouse has been done well. A large diameter window now exists where the goods doors opened onto each floor, served by a hoist. The rail siding and open quayside to the right have been in-filled with new apartments. Canal barges now proceed through the

Taunton Canal lock in the foreground, carrying tourists in place of cargoes. The outer basin and River Parrett locks are far left in this photograph.

218. A new traffic

A little corner of the old industrial past remains adjacent to the inner dock end. Bowerings animal feed factory is, of course, road transport orientated today. Broad and narrow canal boats, brightly painted await their next trip. At least the old dock still has a purpose, and has survived into the twenty first century.

219. The old ship entrance

Bridgwater town is just a short distance further up the River Parrett to the left. In this 2007 photograph, the balance beams of the small barge entrance lock can be seen above the wall of the main ship entrance in the foreground. The former is boarded off but the latter concreted off, out of commission, thus precluding any further sea-going visitations.

220. Bridgwater Bridge

This downstream view to the graceful bridge shows the limit of seagoing navigation on the River Parrett, although barge traffic upstream had once been very important. The wharves beyond the bridge continued to witness much local trade long after the opening of the dock system in 1841. A riverside path connects the town to the old dock entrance.

221. MV RMS SETLARK at Dunball

Some three miles down river from Bridgwater, the Great Western Railway opened Dunball Wharf on the banks of the Parrett. The facility could accept steamers up to about 1,500 tons capacity – a considerable increase over the capabilities of Bridgwater Dock. The wharf fell victim to rail closures in 1962, but in recent decades has seen a revival of trade, with bulk commodities such as salt and aggregates imported. In the 2006 photograph, the L.A.D. type coaster *RMS Setlark* 1,281g/1983 is unloading salt. Barbados registered, yet Estonia operated, she reflects the ever diversifying range of countries involved in the running and registry, of modern merchant ships. The ship's enormous hinged hatch covers are stowed vertically out of the way, leaving the small retractable wheelhouse well and truly obliterated. As the ship is seen sitting on the bottom at low water, it is easy to spot the bow thruster opening, a standard feature today. 'RMS' stands for the line, 'Rhine-Maas-See'. A regular visitor here has been the *Arco Dart* with ballast, described in No.170. Nearby, a little further downstream, BP operated a clean oil distribution depot, recently closed, at Walpole.

222. SS CROWPILL at Combwich

Those little sailing ships were by no means the only ones to squeeze into tight corners to load and unload. Here we see the *Crowpill* 190g/1911, owned in Bridgwater by Sully & Company since 1934, she began life as *Tynesider*. Sully & Co. were an old established firm of coal merchants and ship owners, having made the transition from sail to small steamers in the 1870s. *Crowpill* and the smaller *Enid* continued the business of hauling Welsh coal across the Bristol Channel until scrapped in the early 1960s. Combwich Pill is a small side creek of the River Parrett's west bank some three miles down river from Dunball.

Our voyage around the South West has ended. 'F.W E'

THE BIDEFORD, WESTWARD Ho! & APPLEDORE RAILWAY
MAURICE DART

The act to build a railway from Bideford Quay to Appledore via Westward Ho! and Northam was dated 21st May 1896. The 6 mile standard gauge line opened from Bideford Quay to Northam on 20th May 1901, with the extension to Appledore opening on 1st May 1908. The 7 miles 4 chains long line was worked by train staff and ticket in conjunction with telephone and there were passing loops at Bideford Yard, Abbotsham Road and Westward Ho! The maximum gradient was a stretch of 1 in 40 between Abbotsham Road and Westward Ho! The traffic was mainly passengers but a small amount of goods was also carried. During World War I, the locomotives were requisitioned by the government and the line closed completely on 27th March 1917. To remove the locomotives, temporary rails were laid from Bideford Quay across the road bridge and along the road to Bideford goods yard. All of the rails were lifted shortly afterwards and the carriages were sold by auction at Bideford in April 1921. Using the trackbed, Kingsley Road was built east from Bideford in 1928, and the Somerset & North Devon Coastal Path along the cliffs between Cornborough and Westward Ho! opened on 20th May 1978. Also the sections through the stations at Westward Ho! and at Appledore were converted to roads. Two of the locomotives were on a boat bound for Europe in 1918, but the vessel was torpedoed off the North Cornish coast and the locomotives remain on the seabed.

223.
A two-coach train from Westward Ho! hauled by one of the three locomotives has arrived at Bideford Quay in the 1900s. The locomotives were fitted with protective 'skirts' and American style 'cowcatchers' to conform with the Light Railway Order.

224.
The line was operated by three 2-6-2T locomotives which were built by the Hunslet Engine Company in 1900. These locomotives were named GRENVILLE, KINGSLEY and TORRIDGE. One of them is running along the quay at Bideford in the early 1900s with one of the railway's six carriages on a train from Westward Ho!

225.
The locomotive has run around the train which is ready to depart form Bideford Quay in the early 1900s. The carriages were constructed to a generous width. The 'Kingsley Statue' is in the middle of the background.

226.

One of the locomotives, unfortunately not identified, brings a one coach train past the Kingsley Statue onto the quay at Bideford. The fireman is standing on the side of the engine ready to ring the warning bell which was mounted on the right hand tank.

227.

A locomotive that is stated to probably be KINGSLEY is at Strand Road Halt, on the outskirts of Bideford, with a train for Westward Ho! The coach is one of the American style composite saloons.

228.
The track diagram includes a siding for the gas works at Westward Ho! The railway completed a concert hall on one of the platforms there in 1902, in an attempt to generate more passenger traffic. The name of the town was chosen following the success of a novel, which was published in 1896.

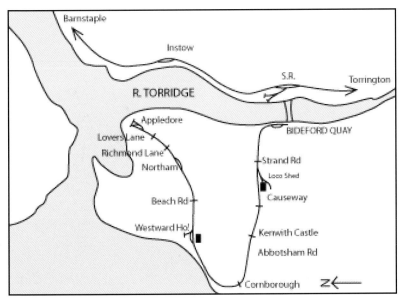

229.
The northern terminus at Appledore is seen on a faded Edwardian postcard. All stations had platforms, except Bideford.

230.
The service interval was usually about one hour during the day, but nearer 30 minutes at busy times when two trains were operated. This timetable is from August 1915.

BIDEFORD, WESTWARD HO! and APPLEDORE.—Bideford, Westward Ho! and Appledore.

Miles	Down.		Week Days.										Sundays.			
		mrn	mrn	non	aft	aft	aft	aft	aft	aft	aft		aft	aft	aft	aft
	Bideford (Quay) ¶..dep.	9 10	1050	12 0	1 10	2 20	3 30	4 52	6 5	7 40	9 15	....	3 0	4 10	6 0	8 10
2¼	Abbotsham Road........	9 20	11 0	1210	2 0	2 30	3 40	5 2	6 15	7 50	9 25	....	3 10	4 20	6 10	8 20
4½	Westward Ho!........	9 28	11 8	1218	1 28	2 38	3 48	5 10	6 23	7 58	9 33	....	3 18	4 28	6 18	8 28
5½	Northam	9 33	1113	1223	1 33	2 43	3 53	5 15	6 28	8 3	9 38	....	3 23	4 33	6 23	8 34
7	Appledore ¶......arr.	9 40	1120	1230	1 40	2 50	4 0	5 22	6 35	8 10	9 45	....	3 30	4 40	6 30	8 40

Miles	Up.		Week Days.										Sundays.			
		mrn	mrn	mrn	mrn	aft	aft	aft	aft	aft	aft		aft	aft	aft	aft
	Appledore ¶......dep.	8 25	9 45	1125	1235	1 45	2 55	4 17	5 30	6 40	8 15	....	2 15	3 5	4 45	7 15
1½	Northam	8 31	9 51	1131	1241	1 51	3 1	4 23	5 36	6 46	8 21	....	2 21	3 41	4 51	7 21
2½	Westward Ho!........	8 36	9 56	1136	1246	1 57	3 6	4 28	5 41	6 51	8 26	....	2 26	3 46	4 56	7 26
4½	Abbotsham Road........	8 42	10 2	1142	1252	2 3	3 12	4 34	5 47	6 57	8 32	....	2 32	3 52	5 2	7 32
7	Bideford (Qhay) ‡ ¶arr.	8 55	1015	1155	1 5	2 15	3 25	4 45	6 0	7 10	8 51	....	2 45	4 5	5 15	7 45

‡ About ¼ mile to L. & S. W. Station.   ¶ "Halts" at Bideford (Strand Road), The Lane, Causeway, and Kenwith Castle, between Bideford (Quay) and Abbotsham Road; Cornborough, between Abbotsham Road and Westward Ho!; Beach Road, between Westward Ho! and Northam; Richmond Road and Lover's Lane, between Northam and Appledore.

Bibliography

Ports of the United Kingdom	Owen, Sir David J.	1939 -	-
Docks & Harbours of Britain	Capt.A.G.Course	1964 –	-
Ports of the World (1985)	Lloyds Press	-	1 850440 395
Coastal & Short Sea Liners	C.V.Waine	1999	0 905184 173
Steam Coasters & Short Sea Traders	C.V.Waine	1976	0 905184 041
The Steam Collier Fleets	J.A.MacRae &		
	C.V.Waine	1990	0 905184 122
British Steam Tugs	P.N.Thomas	1983	0 905184 076
Hartland Quay: Story of a vanished port	M.Nix&M.Myers		0 905818 003
Victorian & Edwardian	B.Greenhill &		
Ships & Harbours	A.Giffard	1978	0 713410 795
Cornwall's Maritime Heritage	Alan Kittridge	2003	0 906294 509
The Ball Clays of Devon & Dorset	Ball Clay Herit.Soc.	2006	1 900147 300
Parrett River Trade	G.Body & R.Gallop	2006	0 946217 254

INDEX

Acknowledgements

I would like to record my thanks and appreciation to all the kind individuals, societies and organisations, who with their time, information and material have so helped with the compilation of this book, in particular: Harold Appleyard, Dr. Philip Armitage, Tim Bass, Hilary Beaumont, Sarah Beighton, Peter Bentley, Hugh St.A.Bowles, John Buckingham, Lesley Byers, David B.Clement, Ian Conday, Rob Cook, Benjamin Dix, Jo Draper, Paul Dyer, Jackie Edwards, Jane Harding, Peter Harman, David Harris, Tom & Jean Haynes, Ren Jackaman, Brian Langworthy, Miss Margaret Lorenz, Duncan Mackenzie, Malcolm McCarthy, Mark Myers, Phil Neumann, Sue Pullen, Richard Samways, Brian Stevens, Vernon Stone, Jessica Vale, Julian Vayne, Pat Warner, Jon Watson, Roger Wedlake, Barrington Weekes, David Whiteside, and Pat Wiggett.

Gratitude goes to Maurice Dart for compiling the Railway section. His contributors were John Alsop, Norman Langridge, Vic Mitchell and Emily Pede, who drew the map.

Photographic sources

Appledore Museum, North Devon Maritime Trust 172 and Edward Blight collection 157; Museum of Barnstaple & North Devon, Peter Harman collection 182,183,184; Blake Museum Bridgwater & Douglas Allen Photography 215,216,222; Braunton & District Museum, Len Baglole collection 187,194; Brixham Heritage Museum 47,48; B.A.Butt 212; David B.Clement collection 32,96 and 31 (Henry Wyke); Combe Martin Museum 201; Dartmouth Museum 58; Devon Record Office, Exeter 35; Exmouth Museum 27,28; Fotoflite 10, 33,43,44,61,74,129,136,159,163,169,170 171, 188; Hartland Quay Museum160; Hayle Foundry Gallery 140; Ilfracombe Museum 196,197; © Judges Postcards Ltd.www.judges.co.uk101,203; Kingsbridge Cookworthy Museum 65,68; Lyme Regis Philpott Museum 25; Duncan Mackenzie collection 85,86,87,88,89,91,94,118,119; Mevagissey Harbour Office 99; © National Maritime Museum,Greenwich 80; Plymouth & West Devon Records Office-Western Morning News Co. PWDRO Accession 1418/E102 75; Padstow Museum, Malcolm McCarthy Collection 148; © Royal National Lifeboat Institution, Poole 147; Royal Institute of Cornwall 152,153; St.Ives Museum & Conley Collection 137,138; Vernon Stone 221; Teignmouth & Shaldon Museum 38,39; Torbay Library Services-reproduced by kind permission of-42; Totnes Image Bank & Rural Archive 50 and Barrington Weekes 52; Watchet Market House Museum 211; Weymouth Museum 4,5,13,14; World Ship Society Photo Library 29,36,57,59,62,71,72,73,142.

Ordnance Survey maps are from the 1930s,
one inch to one mile scale.

MP **Middleton Press**

EVOLVING THE ULTIMATE RAIL **ENCYCLOPEDIA**

Easebourne Lane, Midhurst, West Sussex.
GU29 9AZ Tel:01730 813169

www.middletonpress.co.uk email:info@middletonpress.co.uk

A-978 0 906520 B- 978 1 873793 C- 978 1 901706 D-978 1 904474 E- 978 1 906008

OOP Out of print at time of printing - Please check availability BROCHURE AVAILABLE SHOWING NEW TITLES